18th July 2007

Emma,

For those that work hard, strive for fairness, make commitments that are always beyond the norm & understand respect, the world can truely be 'your oyster'.

Your degree marks a major step on your journey through life.

We are immensely proud of your achievements & hope that you will continue to realise your full potential.

Joan & Ken

(AJ & UK)

BUILDINGS FOR TOMORROW

Paul Cattermole

BUILDINGS FOR TOMORROW

Architecture That Changed Our World

WITH 200 COLOUR ILLUSTRATIONS

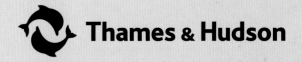
Thames & Hudson

First published in the United Kingdom in 2006 by
Thames & Hudson Ltd,
181A High Holborn, London WC1V 7QX

www.thamesandhudson.com

Text © Paul Cattermole 2006
Photography © The Photographer/Arcaid, www.arcaid.co.uk

Created and produced for Thames & Hudson by
Palazzo Editions Ltd,
15 Gay Street, Bath, BA1 2PH, UK
www.palazzoeditions.com

Book design: Bernard Higton
Picture research: Paul Cattermole
Managing editor: Catherine Hall
Copy editor: Iona Baird

British Library Cataloguing-in-Publication Data
A catalogue record for this book is available from the British Library

ISBN-13: 978-0-500-34228-2
ISBN-10: 0-500-34228-8

Printed and bound in Singapore

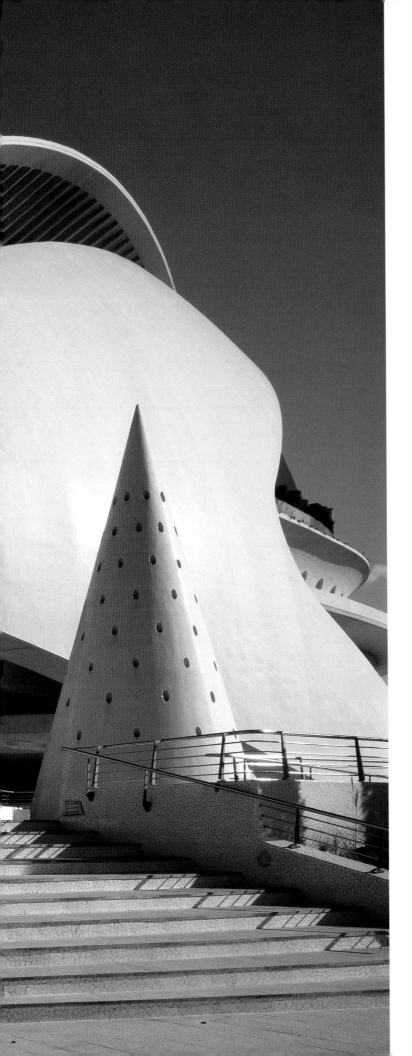

CONTENTS

Architecture is the perfect medium in which to create exciting new visions of the future. Buildings have the power to suggest how the world might look in years to come, their scale immersing the viewer and separating them from the here and now, transporting them to an alternative reality. The line where fact becomes fantasy is being slowly erased as emerging technology, coupled with the will to use it, gathers momentum. Projects that might once have been consigned to the archives on grounds of feasibility are increasingly looking like viable architectural forms.

It would be relatively easy to assemble a volume of unrealized projects from the last one hundred years, in their tantalizing, sketchy glory, their Utopian ideals unconstrained by budgets or even gravity. Similarly, it would not be hard to bring together a catalogue of film sets, a sea of wood and plaster from Hollywood's back lot, or slick computer-generated images, yet these too are but transitory visions, unfettered by niceties such as ergonomics or resistance to the elements. This book takes up the challenge to find the futuristic projects that have actually been built, amazing structures that have been conceived, then developed through to completion. No sketchy details here, for these are not temporary follies for idle pleasure or entertainment, but real architecture that has effectively turned 'science fiction' into science fact. Some of the buildings surveyed are world icons, others hopeful prototypes, and still more should be considered bespoke works of art and craft. A few are so fantastical and photogenic that they have crossed the boundaries between reality and fiction and become film locations in their own right.

It is perhaps unsurprising that this quest to uncover the realities behind the architecture of the future should begin in the US. With its pioneering spirit, manufacturing prowess and abundance of land and natural resources, mid-twentieth-century America provided the ideal breeding ground for innovation and experimentation. These selected works by four highly influential figures in postwar American design serve to illustrate how the technological advances and radical thinking from the late 1930s onwards began to help bring the real and imaginary worlds ever closer. Frank Lloyd Wright, John Lautner, Richard Buckminster Fuller and Eero Saarinen; between these four iconic architects we find a spread of projects produced within a period of just thirty years, but which, when combined, contain all the essential elements of 'buildings of tomorrow'. There is structural ingenuity,

BRAVE NEW DAWN

'Anything one man can imagine,
other men can make real.'

Jules Verne, science-fiction novelist, 1828–1905

Right: The Johnson Wax Building
The double-walled bands of Pyrex tubes that allow diffused light into the interior are illuminated from within at night, emphasizing the streamlined contours of the red brick complex.

engineering know-how, masterful planning and even artistic expression as they take to the air, straddle the landscape or burrow under the ground.

Natural Engineering

Begun in 1936, the Johnson Wax Building in Racine, Wisconsin is a landmark in enlightened corporate office design. It shows how Frank Lloyd Wright's remarkable creativity had remained undimmed in the thirty years since he had fallen from prominence in the architectural community. Together with Falling Water (1935–39), it was this building that re-established him as America's greatest architect in the final two decades of his life.

Wright had been designing office projects for decades, most significantly his 1904 Larkin Building (sadly demolished in 1950). At Larkin, Wright introduced a host of innovations, including the first use of double-glazing, and an inward-facing arrangement of office spaces surrounding a naturally lit central hall. At Johnson Wax he created a double-height, open-plan office, a communal workspace some 61 m long by 37 m wide (200 by 120 ft) ringed by a 5 m (17 ft) deep mezzanine and surrounded by a solid brick outer wall. Wright's ideology concerning the sacred nature of the workspace meant that there were no windows in this outer perimeter, removing distracting views of the world beyond. To provide the required natural lighting, he created bands of glass cornicing running around the circumference of the building, made from stacks of Pyrex tubes similar to the laboratory test-tubes used by the company. The undulating surfaces of the glass-tube panels, sandwiched in steel frames with rubber gaskets in between, distort the light that passes through them, blocking views out while still providing good working light levels. After dark the building can be illuminated to the point where its inhabitants are unsure whether it is night or day.

The most extraordinary elements are the hollow, mushroom-shaped columns that support the building over its three levels. Beginning as 23 cm (9 in.) stems set in steel cups on the ground floor they taper outwards to form discs 5.6 m (18.5 ft) in diameter, linked by lateral beams spanning the 46 cm (18 in.) gaps between them. The effect created in the main workroom is that of a magical soaring forest of dendriform columns that seem to hark back to the lotus capitals of the ancient Egyptian temples of Luxor and Karnak. Remarkably, Wright made no structural calculations

when designing the profiles of these complex forms, using only his own intuition, which was grounded in his careful studies of the staghorn cholla cacti that surrounded his studio in Taliesin West. The columns were constructed in steel formers using expanded steel mesh reinforcing, around which concrete was pumped and vibrated. In order to have the structure approved by the Wisconsin State Building Commission, Wright was obliged to demonstrate the columns' load capacity with a full-scale mock-up. This he duly did and to the astonishment of everyone, except Wright, the slender concrete flower proved capable of supporting a load of over 54.4 tonnes (60 tons), ten times its design load and five times the required safety factor.

Wright's successful fusion of naturally derived structural forms, stylish streamlined aesthetics, innovative materials and a humane working environment make Johnson Wax one of the most successful and futuristic office buildings of the twentieth century. Some fifty years on, the open-plan trading floor and soaring atrium of Richard Rogers's Lloyd's of London (1986) bear witness to Wright's farsighted vision of the future.

Unnatural Interventions

It is only in Frank Lloyd Wright's final major works that we truly come into an era that could be defined as 'science-fiction' architecture. Whereas the Johnson Wax Building is based around a highly functional and rational plan, the Marin County Civic Center is a puzzling work of pure fantasy. More akin to Jabba the Hut's palace than a seat of local government, it was begun in 1957 and completed in 1966, seven years after Wright's death.

Wright was commissioned by the Marin County Board of Supervisors, who had purchased 56 hectares (140 acres) of spectacular countryside on which to build a single centre to bring together thirteen separate local government offices. Whereas Wright's earlier work had been open to constructive criticism by his peers, in later years his isolation from his contemporaries and seclusion in the Taliesin Fellowship, meant that there was no-one sufficiently senior to challenge his ideas. Indeed, any criticism of Wright's proposals was strictly forbidden by his third wife, Olgivanna, who helped maintain a sect-like reverence for him. The result was that his later designs are often considered to lack

The Johnson Wax Building
Sunlight streams into the great communal workroom through the skylights placed between the discs of the mushroom-shaped columns. Wright created a manmade forest canopy that seems straight out of 'Buster' Crabbe's classic 'Buck Rogers' serial (1939). The most important elements in the whole building, the slender tapering legs of the columns pierce the workroom floor, and continue through the carport to ground level.

the intellectual rigour and thorough detailing of his earlier output and this is nowhere clearer than at Marin County.

The concept Wright gave to his clients was of two wings acting as bridges between the hills. The resulting structures appear like vast aqueducts straddling the valleys linked by a rotunda topped with a low dome, 24 m (80 ft) in diameter. With their tiers of arches decreasing as they rise, the wings appear to be powerful structural elements, but this is purely visual as the arches are not loadbearing, the weight of their stucco walls being borne by the concrete floor pads from which they are suspended. Wright seemed to abandon the honest expression of structural functions and the subtle relationships between rectilinear plans and sections, opting instead for random circles and spheres. The modular bricks or concrete blocks that had helped define the scale of his houses, were here replaced by vast pre-cast concrete sections that form the curved roofs, painted with a plastic waterproof membrane in a lurid blue. (Wright originally selected an even less subtle gold, but no metallic paint was capable of enduring such exposure to the elements.) This departure from his own doctrines continued inside, where the communal spaces of Johnson Wax, with their restricted views and air of quiet sanctuary, were replaced with central atriums, referred to as 'malls', that were simply circulation spaces where no meaningful activity took place. The internal focus was further reduced by windows in the façades that gave distracting views out across the valley.

While the Marin Country Civic Center is widely regarded as a poor representation of Wright's architectural legacy, it does provide us with an example of how even great architects, when left unchecked, can stray into territory that is more usually occupied by follies and film sets. The building's sense of unreality was confirmed when it was selected for a prominent role in the film 'Gattaca' (1997), as the futuristic headquarters of the eponymous Gattaca Corporation. There is a certain irony that the film's plot revolves around a fictitious world where DNA analysis determines people's futures at birth, with only superior 'specimens' being permitted to hold rank. The Marin County Civic Center may bear Wright's name but it is lacking the genetic fingerprint of the master's hand in his prime, setting it apart from his finest work.

Marin County Civic Center
The line of the centre cuts across the valley as Wright intended, poking out of the trees like some outlandish Naboo Palace on a 'Star Wars' film set.

The lozenge-shaped slots running down the centre line of each wing form the light wells for the multi-tiered 'malls'.

Earth and Air

John Lautner was a remarkable architect who spent much of his career working on unique private residences in and around Los Angeles. His houses are iconic, not least of all because they seem to crop up so frequently in films, due in part to their proximity to the major studios, but also by virtue of their dramatic locations and unconventional appearance. Lautner possessed a practical mind, having been brought up in the forests of Michigan on the shores of Lake Superior, where he helped his parents build their log cabin at the age of twelve. This physical aspect to his upbringing continued when he was apprenticed to Frank Lloyd Wright firstly at Taliesin East, shortly before moving to Taliesin West, which he helped construct with his own hands. Leaving Wright's employment in 1940 to set up on his own, Lautner's direct connection with materials and the physical aspects of building endeared him to a certain type of client, often in related fields, and so it was common for them to be so closely involved in the design of their homes that it could almost be considered a collaboration.

The Malin House, or Chemosphere (1960), was engineered by Lautner's long-time collaborator, John de la Vaux, and intended as the family home for Leonard Malin, an aircraft electronics engineer. Faced with a tight budget and an almost unbuildable, forty-five-degree sloping site, Lautner's solution was to raise the house on a single concrete pillar, 1.5 m (5 ft) thick and 8 m (27 ft) tall, which was rooted in the hillside, leaving the body of the house to float like a faceted flying saucer. This light touch left the landscape undisturbed, while providing a stable platform upon which to build the octagonal shell. The Chemosphere's entire surface area is exposed, which allowed Lautner to devise air circulation patterns more akin to the aeronautical engineering familiar to his client, than to domestic architecture. Air is drawn into the house through discrete angled vents on the flat underside, passing through the double-walled sides to emerge through grills immediately behind the line of the slanting glass windows. Heating elements are incorporated into these apertures, controlling the temperature of air being admitted into the interior. Through natural convection, the air rises along the curved lines of the ceiling to be expelled through the underside of the Plexiglas dome at its apex, the house effectively drawing air through itself like a jet engine. Yet, despite its futuristic steel envelope, the

Chemosphere (Malin House)

Straight out of the Thunderbirds' Tracy Island, the Chemosphere balances on a single stilt, like a flying saucer temporarily resting on its docking mast. Perhaps the mast should retract after the craft has been launched? Inside, the 360-degree views of Los Angeles are enhanced by the slanting of the glass windows to prevent reflections that might detract from the sensation of floating. The built-in seating covers three sides of the octagonal plan.

house's major internal structural components are made from laminated wood, a material with which both former boatbuilder Vaux and backwoodsman Lautner had good experience. Built just three years after Sputnik was launched, it was almost inevitable the public would brand Chemosphere's octagonal steel form a 'flying saucer', even if it was the most rational, if unconventional, solution to the problems posed by site and budget.

While the Chemosphere seems about to soar off into space, Lautner's Elrod House (1968) is very much a creature of the earth. Built for interior decorator Arthur Elrod, the house occupies a desert clifftop over looking Palm Springs, its low contours giving it a discrete profile on the horizon. When Lautner first visited the site it had been cleared to a dry level crust, but seeing clusters of boulders on surrounding plots he had the client excavate the site to a depth of 3 m (10 ft), which exposed similarly rocky outcrops. These he left in situ, the house being constructed around them, absorbing them into its internal layout. To the approaching road the house presents only a sweeping concrete wall, with a low, covered entrance that looks like a bunker's mouth. This retaining wall hides a private raised garden, which nestles against the house, of which the main external feature is a low conical dome. Over this dome, seven triangular copper panels have been laid, twisted like giant fan blades and glazed between the concrete roof and their raised edges to form clerestory windows. A further two glass 'blades' between the concrete spokes of the roof expose only the grid of their supporting glazing bars.

These skylights give little hint of the dramatic room they illuminate below; the 18 m (60 ft) span of the concrete dome is employed like a tent to create a circular open-plan living space. The wall of one quadrant is cut away and glazed from floor to ceiling to give uninterrupted views over the swimming pool to the twinkling lights of the desert city. A concrete ring beam, 80 cm (2.5 ft) thick, takes the spreading forces of the dome, all beautifully cast and finished by Wally Niewiadomski, a contractor who had previously worked for Frank Lloyd Wright. The effect is one of massive strength, a little like the bomb-proof war room designed by Ken Adam for Stanley Kubrick's 'Doctor Strangelove' (1963). It is so visually striking that the house was used as a location for the James Bond film 'Diamonds Are Forever' (1971), and featured

Elrod House
The earth-coloured roof, bound by sweeping concrete walls, gives little indication of the house sunk into the site, protecting it from the heat of the sun and prying eyes. From the raised inner garden, the form of the house becomes more apparent, with the spread of the copper covers to the openings in the dome rising above a fortress-like external concrete wall.

Sean Connery taking on Bambi and Thumper in Elrod's swimming pool. The use of Lautner's houses as Hollywood's favourite settings blurs the line between cinematic fantasy architecture and the reality of the built environment, as the action flips, scene by scene, from one to the other.

Geodesic Genius

With a career as varied as the designs that he produced, Richard Buckminster Fuller was one of the most unconventional but influential figures in twentieth-century architecture. Having trained as a mathematician at Harvard University, Fuller dropped out before graduating, joining the US Navy in 1917 and serving as a wartime gunboat commander. After leaving the Navy in 1922, he set up the Stockade Building Company specializing in lightweight building materials, but, when this venture failed, he went back to the drawing board and started to design radical new buildings based around the concept of 'four-dimensions'. The fourth dimension in his work was 'time', more specifically the consideration of the long-term implications on the environment, one of the first instances of sustainable thinking in architecture.

From the start, his plans were ambitious, his first patent application being for a four-dimensional tower, a lightweight prefabricated structure that could be delivered anywhere in the world by airship. This was followed by a series of lightweight buildings based on similar principles, which resulted in the famous Dymaxion house of 1929. Unveiled in the Marshall Field Department store in Chicago, the house had a hexagonal plan, with roof and walls constructed from steel, duraluminium and plastic, suspended from a central mast. The term 'Dymaxion' was a combination of 'Dynamic' and 'Maximum Efficiency', terms that Fuller frequently used in lectures on his work. The Dymaxion House led to further lightweight temporary dwellings, including designs used by the US Army to billet airman during World War II, and finally culminated in the 1944 Wichita House, Fuller's first design intended as a permanent home. Developed with the help of the Beech Aircraft Company of Wichita, its round form, domed roof and shiny aluminium skin weighed just 4 tonnes (4.4 tons) and attracted a flood of 38,000 advance orders. But a combination of delays, caused by design refinements and funding problems, eventually confounded Fuller's attempts to get it into

Left: Elrod House
Radiating out from their faceted hub, the concrete blades form a seemingly bomb-proof canopy over the dramatic living room. The space contains the boulders exposed by the site's excavation, an element of the natural landscape brought into the home.

Right: American Pavilion for the 1967 World Exposition
Erected as part of the American Pavilion for the Montreal Expo in 1967, the sphere's original covering was destroyed in a fire, but the durable structure of triangles and hexagons still remains, standing 61 metres (200 feet) tall and 76 metres (200 x 250 feet) wide.

mass-production and only the prototype was ever built. Undeterred, Fuller continued to pursue the Dymaxion principles of obtaining maximum efficiency from the minimum of materials and his persistence finally led to the successful Geodesic Domes that brought him to world prominence.

Taking the triangle as the strongest basic structural form, Fuller devised a means of dividing the surfaces of a sphere into a net of triangular components, patenting the system as 'Geodesics' in 1954. The domes enclosed the maximum possible volume with a minimum surface area and, being self-supporting structures, could be built to almost any size. Fuller even drew up plans for a dome with a 3.2 km (2 mile) wide span that could enclose Manhattan. More tangible examples were soon being constructed across the world, functioning as train depots, glasshouses and even an arctic research station (1975), the dome's uniform loadbearing capabilities making it ideal for standing up to the anticipated snow loads and wind speeds.

A prolific inventor and articulate polymath, Fuller's legacy lives on in the work of Foster, Rogers and Grimshaw, all of whom have taken inspiration from the Dymaxian principles of an architecture based on science and technology, prefabrication, sustainability and environmental awareness. Even the concept of air-deliverable architecture was kept alive in Jan Kaplicky's beautifully drawn design proposals for futuristic weekend retreats prior to forming Future Systems. Fuller's pioneering research, combined with his flair for articulating his ideas, can lay claim to underpinning much of the 'futuristic' architecture of the late twentieth century.

Free Form Thinking

If Buckminster Fuller's geodesic domes were the epitome of a rational and mathematical pursuit of architectural purity, then Eero Saarinen's TWA Terminal must rank as one of the most seductive arguments for pure Expressionism. Commissioned in 1956 by Trans World Airlines (TWA) to act as their private docking space at Idlewild Airport (now John F. Kennedy), the terminal was intended from the outset as the physical projection of the company brand, a concrete expression of their corporate image. Few buildings have ever come as close to capturing the essence of flight as Saarinen's four glorious soaring canopies, cantilevering out from a central hall some 15 m (50 ft) and 96 m (315 ft) long.

The sweeping reinforced concrete roofs and curved entrance voids were perfectly in sync with the stressed metal skins and cavernous air intakes of the first generation of jet airliners that they were built to serve. The basic plan divides the structure into four curved shells, a form that Saarinen explained to his team with the aid of the rind from half his breakfast grapefruit. Pressing down upon its centre, the rind buckled, lifting its edges to create the elliptical voids of the canopies that Saarinen proceeded to fill from floor to ceiling with tinted glass. The transparency of the hall meant that passengers could see the planes landing on the runway as they stood waiting at the ticket desk, turning the whole glamorous business of air travel into a performance piece.

Inside, Saarinen was given free rein to design all the fixtures and fittings, achieving complete uniformity to the scheme. The walls flow into the floors, only to emerge again as flying footbridges arching over the departure lounge. Arrivals boards and reception desks morph seamlessly together as if eroded from pure white stone by centuries of dust-laden winds. The textured, shuttered concrete of the exterior is inside smoothed by the application of flexible sheets of circular white tessera, grouted in to give the sculptural forms a level of curvaceousness unseen in architecture since the demise of Art Nouveau, or since Eric Mendelsohn's Einstein Tower (1926). Saarinen's own engineering expertise meant that he was able to continuously refine his design and maintain complete artistic control.

Though widely celebrated, the terminal's bespoke fittings and organic form have meant that its aesthetic is easily compromised by the insertion of 'foreign' objects such as the highly necessary security and baggage-handling equipment that have gradually appeared since its completion. Its one great failing was the rigidity of the plan, which left no room for expansion in any direction without marring the fine symmetry of the exterior. Sadly Saarinen died the year before the project was completed in 1962, leaving the terminal to act as his lasting monument to organic architecture. Echoes of his influential masterpiece can be found in the leaping forms of Santiago

Calatrava's TGV Station in Lyons (1994) and the undulating, morphing surfaces of Zaha Hadid's Phaeno Science Centre (2005), both of whom prize architecture's capacity for poetry, so eloquently expressed in Saarinen's swansong.

Hidden Depths

Weaving in and out of the six projects surveyed above is the constant power play between the natural and manmade worlds. Nature is clearly a source of perpetual inspiration, capable of being interpreted into remarkable slender concrete columns and swooping shells, a guiding force that can be either adapted, or absorbed, but very rarely ignored. Architects can create buildings that appear to sprout from the earth or bury themselves beneath its surface, simulate the forest canopy or take to the wing.

But then architects have also assimilated the lessons gleaned from man's own engineering achievements, feeding them back into the built environment with houses that perform like jet engines or take on the form of vast mathematical models. They are confident displays of man's own prowess, his triumph over natural forces with the bold application of his material knowledge.

The forty buildings that follow are as radically different from each other as they are from accepted norms, but can be divided loosely into three themes: those that embrace nature, those that reject it and those that seek a seamless combination of the two. This book lays out these differing approaches to the future, exploring their cultural context and design ideologies, while revealing the technology and materials that lie behind their unconventional façades. It is a journey into a parallel world, probing into buildings that seem simply photogenic or flamboyant on the surface, but that invariably prove to have hidden subtleties and greater depths. By peeling back their very different skins to expose their inner workings, the facts behind the architectural fantasy can start to emerge.

These forty buildings give an exhilarating account of the architecture that has changed our world.

TWA Terminal at JFK Airport
The wilful, free-flowing forms of the cantilevered canopies produce fantastical shapes over the approaching passengers, especially at dusk when the low beams of the sun turn their silhouettes into black Picasso abstractions. Where the four wings meet, the structure touches the ground with V-shaped columns so curved that they seem to be growing out of the earth. The raised surface patterns of the planks used as shuttering give the surface a lively, crafted texture.

OTHER WORLDS

'Imagination creates reality.'

Richard Wagner, composer and theorist, 1813–83

The Ancient, the Organic and the Alien

Our architecture is our identity. Our daily lives – working, sleeping and playing – are spent either in or among buildings. They form the physical fabric of our world. Ever since man left the caves and began to build shelters of his own, he has been responsible for weaving that fabric, for shaping his environment. Into these forms he has poured his material knowledge, his ingenuity and his aspirations. Great civilizations have come and gone, leaving only their architecture as a clue to their daily routine, technical prowess and spiritual beliefs.

It is no coincidence then, that film-makers attempting to draw us into fictional worlds should concentrate so studiously on the creation of a physical architecture to make their illusion complete. Ever since Fritz Lang created the dark, brooding towers of 'Metropolis' in 1927, cinematic science-fiction has made the assiduous development of convincing environments its modus operandi. The completely artificial worlds of George Lucas's sprawling 'Star Wars' epics are the culmination of decades of technical refinement, where each species has its own clearly defined culture, ceremonies, weapons, history and even religion. No detail is considered too small in this quest for total simulation of an alternative reality.

But when the final credits roll and the lights come on, the audience is back once more in a world populated with everyday buildings and punctuated by familiar landmarks, all linked by well-trodden paths. Or perhaps not.

In this chapter we find examples of an architecture less ordinary, buildings that seem to have leapt from the silver screen and landed in our midst. This is architecture's wild side; the daring, experimental aspect to a discipline that normally houses us in the most mundane surroundings. It is human fantasy let loose.

Many of these buildings are unique, beautifully sculpted one-offs that owe their forms to the vision of the craftsmen who laboured over them. They embody that nineteenth-century concept originated by Wagner, of the 'gesamtkunstwerk', quite literally 'a total work of art'. Their illusory powers are maintained by the banishment of all familiar everyday objects, replacing them with carefully conceived alternatives, like so many props littered about a stage. Without any references to tie us firmly into reality, the illusion begins to take hold, for if the fantasy were to be complete there can be no distractions. The perfect dreamscape is easily ruined by cracks in the walls.

Historically the more detailed the vision, the more expensive the project, so the 'science-fiction' home has traditionally been a luxury of the wealthy. In the nineteenth century it was only the Victorian super-rich who could choose to recreate the medieval idyll, building vast castellated mansions and surrounding themselves with Arthurian imagery and handmade objects in a vain attempt to drown out the clamouring mechanized reality of the Industrial Revolution. Such richly detailed environments seem distant, being out of reach of the majority, as do the contemporary houses designed by Bart Prince and Kendrick Kellogg, which require a level of patronage that is beyond most pockets. But in Dr. Eugene Tsui's house we find a home every bit as removed from daily reality as those Victorian Gothic fantasies, but one that could conceivably be self-built by the modern-day everyman applying trowels of render to carved blocks of polystyrene and sheets of plywood.

It was Modernism with its love of mechanization that created the accepted vision of twentieth-century modernity, rejecting applied ornament and embracing clean white concrete walls and precisely machined steel and chrome surfaces. The style finds favour still, but man frequently rebels against the sterile geometric perfection of its white boxes, expressing a longing for a world that is as rich in colour, pattern and texture as nature itself. With modern technology at their disposal, architects seemingly now have the freedom to create whatever forms they wish and are able to abandon the constraints of squares and rectangles to sculpt organic domes, distorted spheres and flowing lines. Beams have become bones, roofs turned to shells and galleries morphed into alien metal flowers. Even the skyscraper (traditionally the most rectilinear of monoliths) has been softened with curves, styled as trees, and encrusted with decorative motifs, while stretching to ever-greater heights.

But where do all these projects find their inspiration, their inner logic, their raison d'être? Are they really just works of mad fiction, arbitrary forms tacked together with the help of today's technology? No. It would be a mistake to write them off as pure whimsy, acts of sheer folly or fantasy, for beneath their undulating curves and unworldly façades, there lurks technical wizardry, cultural resonance and even sustainable logic.

This is real architecture, but not as we know it.

TSUI HOUSE

Ask any contemporary architect whether a building should respond to its environment, take account of the pressing issue of sustainability and address the ecological imperative, and you are guaranteed an affirmative answer. These are, after all, accepted as conventional wisdoms in the profession today. The Tsui House is a startling example of how these conventions need not necessarily lead to conventional architecture, and that environmentally conscious design can be something far freer than the dry laboratory study of optimum surface areas, calculated solar gain and thermal mass. There is clearly room for intuitive experimentation and artistic expression, colour, texture and form.

The house Dr. Eugene Tsui has created for his parents looks as though it was not so much built as sculpted. Sitting on a perfectly ordinary street, with white, orthogonal concrete neighbours on either side, the Tsui House is a visual delight of sweeping curves and tactile surfaces. If it suggests the sea, then this is because its overall structure is based on that of the Tardigrade, a hardy microscopic marine invertebrate discovered in 1773 that is capable of living in almost any environment in the world, from the Arctic to the Tropics. The walls are constructed from 'Rastrablocks', blocks of recycled Styrofoam and cement, which were glued together, pinned with reinforcing bars and then filled with concrete. The curving roof was built up with layers of stressed wood sheeting, sprayed with concrete, then textured and painted. This solid combination of materials produced a structure that is both highly insulated and, when combined with the oval plan and four-degree lean of the walls, earthquake-proof. With its curving plan and continuous moulded parabolic roof, the house has the appearance of a colossal shell, once inhabited by a prehistoric creature before being washed up in a quiet Californian suburb.

From the road, the Tsui House looks like it might be Aqua Marina's weekend retreat, with Troy Tempest's Sting Ray parked in the garage. The main tower, with its gold render and porthole windows, looms like an organic diver's helmet above the white rendered mass.

Right: The side elevation reveals the pronounced ridges of the subsurface tubes running, rib-like, across the arched roof, with the radial fins of the oculus below.

ARCHITECT	Dr. Eugene Tsui
LOCATION	Berkeley, California, USA
CREATED	1993–95

Soaring protectively above the front door like the bony armoured collar of a Triceratops, the raised ridges of the sub-surface radiating tubes form a dramatic fin that presents a large surface area to the sun's rays.

The prehistoric parallels prove to be more than superficial, as the architect found further inspiration in the Dimetradon, an early dinosaur from the Permian period, whose most prominent feature was a sail-like fin running down the length of its back. Palaeontologists speculate that this fin was used to heat the reptile's blood by presenting the maximum surface area to absorb the sun's rays, though it could equally have been used to cool down by radiating heat if required. Tsui adopted this principle by covering the roof with a series of water-filled, flexible plastic tubes, clearly visible as ridges under the top layer of gold-painted render. Using the high specific heat capacity of water, the tubes heat up slowly during the day, and radiate the stored warmth at night. The banked earth of the garden outside, rising 1.5 m (5 ft) against the walls, adds to the stability and thermal mass of the house. The garden is filled with hardy native Californian plants that require little watering, having adapted to this dry environment. Tsui has successfully approached the home not as a Corbusian 'machine for living', but as a living organism, capable of regulating its own internal temperature using systems that are over 150 million years old.

Inside, the house's most dramatic feature is the 10 m (33 ft) high central rotunda, with its spiralling ramp to the upper floor passing a 5 m (16 ft) diameter oculus that floods the space with natural light. The oculus is decorated on the outside with a halo of blue and gold fins that seem poised to spin, like so many organic turbine blades, propelling the house back out to sea. The ramp's underlying structure of Douglas fir timbers is suspended from gold-tipped steel cables attached to the ceiling. The seating in the rotunda is built-in, like much of the furniture in the house, using the same materials as the walls, giving the interior a structural uniformity, as though it has been organically grown around the occupants.

Tsui has written lengthy explanations of the house's design logic, imbuing each element with its own structural or symbolic significance. Yet it is not the resourceful logic of the house that sticks in the mind, but the air of joyful freedom that is so evident in its flowing forms and playful details. The Tsui house is one of the purest examples of how architecture can become a vehicle for self-expression, a triumph of imagination and ingenuity over the mundane. It works, it sustains and it gives pleasure.

Left: The oculus, constructed from an acrylic dome surrounded by steel reinforced fibreglass, peeps over the lip of the ramp's textured plaster banister. At night the interior is illuminated by a ring of recessed ceiling lights.

Above: The curved seating at the base of the rotunda forms the heart of the house. Wrapped by the spiralling ramp and with its floor beneath ground level, it is cool, quiet and secure.

Right: The whiplash tendril lines of the ramp curve around to form the womb-like seating area at its heart. Its pleasingly handmade surface incorporates industrial objects, such as the steel colanders embedded to form the base for the star-shaped ventilation grills.

Museums are generally dedicated to the continued preservation of valuable artefacts, objects of cultural and historical significance that have outlived their time and need to be sympathetically housed and carefully maintained in order that future generations may use them for reference. The Museum of Fruit in the Yamanashi Prefecture of Japan is an exception to this rule, being designed to house exhibits that are perishable and cannot be sustained in their original form, their flesh swelling with the seasons and withering away if not consumed near the time of harvest. True, they can be preserved in sugar or alcohol but these tinned, jarred or dried remnants are only shadows of their former voluptuous incarnations. Only their seeds remain the same, lying dormant until the opportunity arises to sprout. It was then perhaps a logical step for Itsuko Hasegawa, Japan's foremost female architect, to use the forms of these enduring seeds as the basis for her museum design.

The museum sits in the Kofu Basin area, which yields the biggest crops of deciduous fruits anywhere in Japan. The idea of celebrating these essential foodstuffs and elevating them to a curatorial curiosity seems peculiarly Japanese, but given the importance of the crop to the local economy, it should perhaps not be seen as surprising. After all, no one bats an eyelid at Stoke-on-Trent's museum galleries packed full of pottery and fine china.

MUSEUM OF FRUIT

ARCHITECT	Itsuko Hasegawa
LOCATION	Yamanashi, Japan
CREATED	1993–96

Left: The spartan sloping site next to the Fuefuki river gave the new museum an unworldly air, the deformed shapes of the various elements glowing like alien forms emerging from the fertile soil.

Above: The tight, hard glazed form of the Greenhouse's shell seems half-buried in the earth, like a seed pod trying to take root.

The roof terrace restaurant sits under the summit of the curving ribs of the Workshop 'cage'. The elevated position on the vineyard slopes affords spectacular views of Mount Fuji in the distance.

Like some space-age colony on Mars, the Museum of Fruit is a delicate collection of steel and glass pods, skeletal ammonites clustered on a barren landscape. When first completed, the immediate environment seemed like a hostile planet's surface, but this was only temporary, as the various plant species growing across the site transformed it into a living exhibit.

The first of the three museum components is the Greenhouse, a suitably high-tech canopy with a glazed steel structure sprouting from a hub at ground level and rising in ever-increasing arches to reach a maximum height of 20 m (66 ft) before curving back down to the other side. In profile, the structure is a deformed sphere, with one half roughly hemispherical, while the other is deliberately flattened. The irregularity lends the form a more naturalistic appearance, as perfect machined symmetry rarely exists in the natural world. Inside the house is a lush canopy of tropical fruit plants and trees, like some primeval Eden caught in a twenty-first-century bubble.

The Greenhouse is linked to the second element, the flattened dome of the Events Space, by an underground gallery that doubles as a tunnel. Visitors emerge from the subterranean exhibits into a stepped performance area with a grove of columns at its centre that shoot up and over their heads to create a steel forest canopy. The canopy ends in fully glazed walls that give the impression that it is floating. The space is theatrical, like a throne room of some far-flung kingdom where a fruit-filled monarch might hold court.

The final element is the Workshop Building, a four-storey block with a rectangular plan surrounded by elliptical balconies that almost touch the swelling lattice that envelopes it like a cage. This is also a deformed solid, but left unglazed to form a giant pergola over which creeping fruit-laden lianas have been planted. The building houses offices, educational kitchen facilities and, at its top, a restaurant.

All these elements were designed and built to exacting Japanese codes to resist damage by the earthquakes that plague the region. Engineers Ove Arup took the opportunity to use the latest GSA dynamic stress modelling software to test strength, buckling and to minimize glass breakage in the event of seismic activity. With their help, Hasegawa has created a resilient and futuristic setting in which the importance of fruit can be presented to fertile young imaginations.

The outstretched high-precision ribs of the Greenhouse seem to echo the primeval tropical fronds it contains.

The swelling stem of the Events Space roof forms the dramatic apex of the stage area where lectures and performances are given.

ARCHITECT	Niall McLaughlin Architects
LOCATION	Northamptonshire, England
CREATED	1996

Buildings can be as much about the memory of a place as of the here and now. This small but highly expressive project ably demonstrates how an architect can make a structure resonate with its surroundings on multiple levels.

Niall McLaughlin's client was a female photographer who specialized in recording water insects and together they collaborated to create this highly original approach to a garden studio. The site was a pond at the bottom of the client's garden, looking out over farmland where once a World War II American airbase had stood. Blackened B-24 bombers flying missions to aid resistance fighters in occupied Europe were replaced postwar by massive concrete works intended to serve as a nuclear missile base. The site was eventually abandoned in the 1960s, leaving it littered with military debris, including a dismantled bomber buried just below the surface. It was the twin strands of echoing a war-scarred, injured landscape (akin to the dark paintings of the German artist Anselm Kiefer that McLaughlin admires), and of bringing the photographer's lens to the water's edge that gave rise to 'The Shack'.

The seemingly freeforms of The Shack are a direct result of the design process. The builder, Simon Storey, only agreed to construct The Shack without working drawings, giving him the necessary leeway to interpret the 1:10 scale models and collages

Left: The once stagnant pond was filtered and then oxygenated with plants to encourage the wildlife to return to become the photographer's muse. The Shack functions as studio, hide and family retreat, complete with reading nook and sauna.

Below: Perched with its wings outstretched, the bird-like form of the Shack, its 'beak' projecting from the duel purpose lantern/observation tower, looks as though it has just come to rest at the pond's edge.

THE SHACK

McLaughlin and the client had created. The structure centres around rendered concrete block walls sitting on a concrete raft, from which radiates a wooden deck that hovers above the pond's surface. The Shack is roofed with a complex wing, constructed from plywood and fibreglass over a thin steel girder frame, in a form that bears a strong resemblance to the menacing boomerang shape of a B-2 Spirit stealth bomber. While the US Government covertly spent on estimated US $23 billion (£15 billion) on the clandestine development of the B-2, this stealthy waterside creature was realized on a more modest budget of £15,000.

Aeronautical imagery aside, the building can be readily interpreted as a combination of both insect and bird forms. The large outstretched canopy seems to echo the technique used by wading birds of spreading their wings to shade the water's surface, making it easier for them to spot their prey. The external shades that run along the eastern side are made from thin sheets of perforated galvanized steel, supported near their tips by steel rods that dart down into the water next to the stepping-stones leading to the entrance to the sauna. The staggered series of steel plates shade the glazed roof of the main room, forming a seemingly articulated spine with the visual fragility of a dragonfly's tail. Beneath the glazing, a series of polycarbonate baffles further control the light coming into the room below. The lightness of the minimal structure means that it becomes animated by the wind, increasing the variety of rippling light effects that reflect and refract around the interior.

It was this desire to capture the myriad light effects and bring the photographer closer to her subject that kept informing the design decisions. The deep-framed square windows in the main wall act as little niche studios where found objects can be arranged and photographed, illuminated by the reflected light from the water outside.

The Shack is a fine example of how a small domestic building with a modest budget can still become an exercise in artistic exploration, leaving behind the hackneyed vocabulary of conventional sheds and gazebos, and adding a highly contemporary chapter to the history of garden architecture. McLaughlin has shown himself to be highly adept at working at a small scale and has since gone on to produce an equally successful freeform bandstand for the famous De La Warr Pavilion in Bexhill-on-Sea (2001), as well as several award-winning private houses.

The perforated steel sheet used to form the serried shades is like an architectural rendering of the fine gauze of the dragonfly's wings, making reference to the photographer's subject matter.

The steel structure and polycarbonate baffles in the ceiling produce a dramatic striped effect of light and shadow down the walls. Light falls across the constantly changing compositions of found objects that the photographer client places on the windowsills.

ARCHITECT	Timo & Tumamo Suomalainen
LOCATION	Helsinki, Finland
LAUNCHED	1968–69

TAIVALLAHTI CHURCH

It is worth remembering that Christianity was once very much an underground religion, its followers widely persecuted and its places of worship concealed for fear of discovery. From the secret depths of the catacombs of Rome to Ethiopia's Lalibela churches sunken into hillside ravines, the faithful have learnt how to express their beliefs quietly in often subterranean circumstances.

In twentieth-century Helsinki it was not fear of reprisals but concerns for the urban fabric of the city that brought a new chapter to the architecture of underground worship. The Suomalainen brothers' design for the Taivallahti Church, often referred to as 'The Church of the Rock', was the winning entry to an open competition in 1960, but construction did not actually begin until 1968, due to internal arguments over the need for a new church in the area.

The square, long a place of communal recreation, is dominated by a rocky outcrop standing some 8 to 13 m (26 to 43 ft) above the surrounding streets and surrounded by apartment blocks, many of them eight storeys high. It was the architects' concerns to ensure that the church did not dominate these houses, or encroach upon the open space so valued by city-dwellers, that led them to sink the building into the ground. The structure was hewn out of the rock, and quarried to the same depth as the surrounding streets, with the displaced material being used to build a curtain wall around the perimeter. This curtain wall acts as a sound barrier that prevents people enjoying the open space above from disturbing the services below, fulfilling the requirement that the populace should not lose their valued local amenity.

The rock walls of the church, while providing natural insulation with their mass, also required small underfloor trenches at their base to drain away the water that slowly seeps out. The architects specified that the rock should be left rough hewn by blasting, rather than carefully quarried. This rich undulating texture not

Right: Clergymen emerging from the vestry tunnel are treated to the inspiring sweep of the dome with its halo of radiating concrete beams above their waiting congregation.

Above: From street level, the dome can just be seen discretely rising from its outer ring of rough-hewn rock. Unlike the inner wall, the outer blocks are not held together by mortar, but stacked and retained with steel bindings to create a more natural effect.

Right: The underside of the reinforced concrete dome is covered with a soundproofing membrane, then sheathed with 20 mm (0.8 in.) wide strips of copper nailed to the structure. The shimmering ceiling resembles the orb of the sun, casting warm reflections on the congregation below.

The control room provides the ideal
vantage point for appreciating the
structure's drama. The beautiful
striped effect of light and shadow that
the beam construction affords can be
seen in the centre.

only gives character, but also improves the acoustics when the church is used as concert venue. The inner rock walls are bound together with concealed mortar joints to create a more natural extension to the rock itself.

The 180 concrete beams that support the dome provide a 360-degree halo of light to illuminate proceedings. In a touch reminiscent of Neolithic stone circles, the internal arrangement has been carefully considered so that the usual time for morning worship coincides with direct sunlight falling onto the altar wall. The beams vary in length to provide the connection between the precise geometry of the dome, some 24 m (79 ft) wide, and the irregular circumference of the natural rockface. The overall effect is at once both futuristic and traditional, with the saucer-like dome lightly tethered to the rock of ages past.

From the road, the low-lying concrete entrance gives an initial impression of the mouth of a bunker, but this image is quickly

dispelled as the visitor enters the glowing copper-lined interior. The coarse rock face, rough hewn rock walls, shuttered concrete pews and altar are warmed by the shimmering copper cladding on the underside of the gallery, which reflects the rich purple of the upholstery on the pews. Situated in a densely populated urban area, the church was designed for both worship and entertainment, with a purpose-built dais for a choir to the left of the altar and space for an orchestra in front. A soundproofed

control room at the rear of the upper gallery can be used for TV and radio recordings, broadcasting services to an even wider audience.

The Suomalainen brothers' solution has provided a suburb with a cultural hub and place of worship without depriving them the luxury of open space. With the well-considered intervention of the Taivallahti Church, Christianity has gone to earth with aplomb.

Founded in 1937, the Solomon R. Guggenheim Foundation is an American institution with an inherently European flavour, its collection based around works from the first half of the twentieth century by the avant-garde artists of the 'Old World'. Paradoxically it took the Foundation's American Director, Thomas Krens, to return a substantial segment of the Guggenheim's collection to its continental origins, reconnecting it with its roots and in so doing, revitalizing the fortunes of Spain's fourth largest city and accelerating the demand for iconic architecture worldwide.

Coastal Bilbao had long been a powerhouse of the shipbuilding industry, but with the decline of the fishing fleet and reduction in trawler numbers, the regional government took radical steps to help the city's economy diversify and survive. It began by commissioning high-profile architects to build a brand new transport infrastructure; Norman Foster designing its underground system, Santiago Calatrava the airport terminal and Michael Wilford the railway station. But what it lacked was a cultural icon that would cause the tourists to disembark on its plethora of shiny new platforms. The need to bring in the crowds led it to court the attentions of the Guggenheim's Thomas Krens in 1991, offering him a former wine-bottling warehouse in the city centre for conversion into a gallery. Krens saw little potential in this cramped,

GUGGENHEIM BILBAO

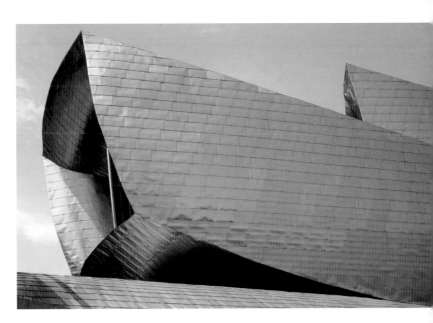

Left: The freeform curves of the titanium-clad volumes are a direct translation of Gehry's original models, as though the architect has been able to shape the building with his own hands.

Above: The elongated skylights of the temporary exhibition space reach out towards the city, bearing their skin of lock-seamed titanium plates, only 0.38 mm (1/64 in.) thick.

ARCHITECT	Frank Gehry
LOCATION	Bilbao, Spain
CREATED	1991–97

inflexible building, with its low ceilings and obtrusive columns, but he spotted his ideal site the very next day on his morning jog. Lying next to the river Nervion, the derelict zone was partially occupied by warehouses and bordered by a road bridge and a railway line, but in this site Krens could see the perfect setting for a gallery that could respond to the city and form a gateway to the business and historic quarters. The city bureaucrats agreed, taking just a week to approve his proposal. Within a few short months of Krens's perambulatory epiphany, a closed competition had been held between Frank Gehry, Arata Isozaki and Coop Himmelblau. Gehry was pronounced the winner and commissioned to build the Guggenheim's new European flagship.

Gehry's design began as a series of freehand sketches that he made standing on the riverbanks overlooking the site. Back in his studio he transformed the energetic lines into hundreds, if not thousands, of models, created by folding, twisting and crumpling paper and card to create the apparently random forms that crystallized to become a building. The next step – a quantum leap in building design – was only made possible by the extensive use of CAITA, a French computer program borrowed from the aviation industry that had previously been used to design the Mirage jet fighter and the Boeing 777. Gehry's physical models were translated into the virtual world by means of a laser that scanned and digitized their curves, turning them into three-dimensional computer models that could be scaled up to full size. From this data, the engineers and contractors could generate plans and sections with relative ease, the automatic plotting of the inter-related components allowing the designers to quickly alter one element while the computer adjusted all of the others in turn.

The basic structure is formed from steel I-section beams that are used to construct a grid of sections approximately 3 m (9.8 ft) square. Each of the components was cut by computer-controlled numeric cutters (CNC), using the data straight from the architect's model. The sections were bolted, rather than welded together, as the holes could be pre-drilled to an unparalleled degree of accuracy. The building was divided into contoured layers and the numbered sections brought to the site for assembly, like a gigantic Meccano set. A projecting layer of curved steel tubes attached to the I-beam skeleton smoothed its faceted edges into graceful forms. To these contours were fixed vertical steel bars and over the bars, the final layer of overlapping titanium sheets, held by stainless-steel screws, created the building's shimmering skin. The high level of co-operation between architect, engineer and contractor, simultaneously sharing the data, resulted in a finished building that was delivered on time and on budget (£44 million) without losing any of its sculptural panache along the way.

Gehry's innovative architectural approach produced one of the world's most recognizable signature buildings, and fuelled an unprecedented rise in landmark projects intended to emulate the subsequent urban regeneration with which the gallery is credited. That this phenomenon is now universally referred to as 'the Bilbao effect' is perhaps the project's highest accolade, bearing testimony to Krens's curatorial foresight and Gehry's unique Californian flair.

Left: The gallery's interior is no less unconventional – mirroring the billowing forms of the exterior, but finished in limestone and white plaster.

Right: Following the lines of the river, the gallery rises up like a metallic apparition, a haunting echo of Bilbao's fading shipbuilding heritage, with its multiple bows.

Caught by the rays of the late
afternoon sun, the cedar shingles
of the enveloping canopy take on
the appearance of beaten gold leaf,
blending with the red hues of the
copper-roofed 'pods'.

America's West Coast can boast some of the most unusual private houses in the world; the combination of plentiful land and clients with deep pockets provides architects with an opportunity to explore design avenues that would otherwise be closed to them. In Bart Prince's own words, 'We live in a time that allows us to do virtually anything where design is concerned.'[1] The Price House is a dazzling example of how that artistic freedom can be used to answer a client's brief without resorting to hackneyed historical forms or sacrificing any of the structural legibility.

The house takes the form of three 'pods', loosely semicircular in plan, arranged one behind the other in an overlapping line rising behind an enveloping freeform exterior shell. This shell shields the 'pods' from prying eyes on the public road outside. The shell is supported on a wooden framework with some steel reinforcements over which an undulated mass of cedar shingles have been laid to create an irregular surface of swirling, bulging lines. Shingles are a common roofing material for the region, but Prince has transformed the regular slats from a flat surface covering into a three-dimensional medium. The process of building such an unusual structure began with the hand-drawn plans, (all done in pencil on Mylar without any recourse to computers), which gave an initial indication of how the shingle patterns would appear. Prince flew to the house for weekly site meetings with foreman Eric Johnson to discuss how each section of shingles should be applied, allowing the craftsmen some leeway for interpretation while still retaining overall artistic control. In places the shingles are layered ten to fifteen deep, turning the surface into a giant wooden contour map that seems to be billowing in the fresh ocean breeze.

Inside, the house is dominated by the structural elements that define its form. In order to free up the ground floor, Prince chose to support each of the three living 'pods' on single central columns, perhaps best described as 'trees'. Rooted in separate concrete floor pads (allowing them to sway independently in the event of an earthquake), these trunks rise to ceiling height before branching out in all directions to form the floor of the pods above. The beams then extend up the sides to form the walls, finally turning back on themselves to link again with the central trunk to support the roof. The components are all strips of fir some

PRICE HOUSE

The U-shaped ground floor surrounds the south-facing swimming pool, a private wonderland bridged in two places to allow easy access to the lower living rooms.

ARCHITECT	Bart Prince
LOCATION	Corona Del Mar, California, USA
CREATED	1984–89

Left: Prince's use of laminated timber extends to the bespoke furniture within the house, including this desk with its integrated reading lamp enclosed within a hooded serpentine form.

Below: With its blue translucent plastic treads illuminated from beneath, the undulating shingle wall of this internal staircase shows the extent to which Prince has fused traditional and modern materials to form his own vocabulary.

2 cm (0.78 in.) thick, laminated together to form members with a section of 7.5 x 23 cm (3 x 9 in.). This method allowed for less wastage and longer lengths. The wood takes all the strain, the only structural additions being the steel plates inserted into the nearly perpendicular junctions between the members. These are pinned together with stainless-steel nuts and bolts, the heads of which are further protected from the proximity of the sea air by turned wooden stoppers. Most spectacular of the three columns is the spiral staircase that leads to the master study, an intricate composition that could so easily double as a central fixture in Captain Nemo's 'Nautilus', diving 20,000 leagues under the sea. Although the structure is almost entirely made from wood, its turned stoppers and perforated steel knees have that confident, muscular quality of Victorian Gothic engineering with its clusters of rivet heads and solid, tangible components.

Each of Prince's houses is very much a one-off, and here he has provided his client with a richly textured jewel box from which to enjoy the ocean views. To the casual observer, Prince's world may be one of fantastical creations, but it is one that he has proved to be both structurally rational and eminently buildable.

The laminated wooden treads of the spiral staircase are visually lightened by strips of copper set into their leading edges. The hollow centre provides service and wiring ducts while steel brackets anchor it to the concrete base.

TJIBAOU CULTURAL CENTRE

The clusters of towers, strung out along the line of the main complex, make for a convincing village analogy, especially when seen side-by-side with the traditional Kanak huts that form part of the open-air display.

The conundrum that faces architects, artists and film-production designers alike when set the challenge of physically realizing our future, is how much to borrow from the past. For many, this is a straightforward 'cut and paste' exercise, taking existing historic or contemporary elements and combining or exaggerating them to create a distortion of both past and present. But this method does little justice to the essence of a culture's architecture, its underlying ethos or the spiritual significance of its component parts. Designers would do well to follow Renzo Piano's example when it comes to imagining a future that has a genuine resonance with the past.

The late Jean-Marie Tjibaou was the leading figure in the campaign for international recognition of the Kanak culture, which was marginalized and ignored by the westernized agenda of the French government. Even before his death in 1989, Tjibaou's advanced political negotiations meant that the idea for a purpose-built centre to preserve and sustain the Kanak culture was already in place. The centre's site, on a narrow peninsula extending out into the blue lagoon, is as significant as its purpose. It was here

in 1975 that the Melanesia 2000 Festival was held, considered to be one of the turning points in the New Caledonian Independence Movement's struggle with the French government. An international competition was announced, from which Renzo Piano's design was selected by a jury that included both the French President François Mitterrand and Tjibaou's widow, Marie-Claude – a clear indicator that a high level of political consensus had been reached.

Piano's design took inspiration from many sources in Kanak culture while avoiding any direct replication. The centre's most distinctive feature is a series of towers, modelled largely on the 'Great Houses' of the Kanak, the most important buildings in their

ARCHITECT	Renzo Piano Building Workshop
LOCATION	Nouméa, New Caledonia, Melanesia
CREATED	1991–98

villages. In the original structures, curved members, made from palm saplings, meet at the top and are lashed together before being thatched. Piano deliberately left the ends of his towers open, signifying that the culture whose artifacts they exhibit is still expanding and evolving, rather than being a remnant of history. This important detail, together with their open backs, makes the towers a resolutely modern interpretation, crisply constructed with laminated iroko ribs joined by stainless-steel tie rods. The iroko, a naturally resilient African hardwood, will weather in time to silvery grey and blend in with the steel ties and silvery trunks of the surrounding palms. By facing them into the prevailing winds that blow across the lagoon, wind tunnel tests have demonstrated that the open tops aid the natural ventilation system of the towers, as the air passing over their upper edges sucks stale air upwards. The outer cladding also has a system of louvres so that air can be allowed to pass through the interior if cooling is required.

The towers are used for special exhibits, such as lofty spiritual carvings, and as lecture theatres and performance spaces. They are joined to the main complex, a lower-lying, one-storey building that houses the main educational facilities, offices and further exhibition spaces. The open staves and cross-braced elements of the towers, together with the low profile of the other facilities, enables the structures to resist the 230 km/h (143 mph) cyclone winds that occasionally blow across this tropical paradise.

With its careful blend of cultural heritage and modern detailing, the Tjibaou Cultural Centre is a prime example of architecture that responds to both its natural and historical context, providing future generations of the Kanak with a truly spiritual home.

Below left: Circular in plan, with the obliquely sliced ribs graduating to a height of 28 m (92 ft), the seemingly incomplete towers, or 'cases', offer a metaphor for the work of representing the Kanak's continuing heritage.

Below right: The Jinu House (one of the towers that forms part of the first 'village') contains spiritual works of art donated by cultures from across the Pacific, their elongated forms accommodated by the inclined roof.

Right: The circular sloping roofs of the exhibition spaces are cradled by the vertical wooden ribs, like fingers stretched to the sky. Visual density is created by double rows of ribs, the outer row being curved to deflect the wind while the straight inner ones support the flat interior walls.

Australia has more than its fair share of natural wonders with dramatic coastlines, sprawling vistas and vibrant reefs that have all contributed to its multi-billion-dollar tourist industry. Perhaps the most audacious attempt to capture this essence of Australia and bring it straight into the home came in the 1960s, when maverick architect Eugene Van Grecken chose to site his revolutionary design on the sandstone cliffs above Bayview. Here, some 153 m (502 ft) above sea level hovers his masterpiece, the Spaceship House.

This is no modest country dwelling, but a true feat of engineering virtuosity so far ahead of its time that it was not officially approved by local government simply because no qualified engineer was willing to sign the paperwork. Australian attitudes to daring structures have changed since the fraught but ultimately successful Sydney Opera House was completed in 1973 (just forty minutes drive away), but the Spaceship still remains the largest freeform concrete structure in the southern hemisphere. No mean claim for a privately built domestic building.

The elliptical-domed concrete roof, some 25 m wide by 20 m across (83 by 68 ft), rests on eleven boomerang shaped pillars and is held on only by gravity. The tips of the pillars are covered in 5 cm (2 in.) thick neoprene pads that allow the roof to slide back and forth as it expands and contracts in the fierce Australian sun. The sweeping curves of the beams and dome make for a far more sympathetic and organic intervention onto such an openly natural landscape than any Modernist cube could have hoped to achieve. There is that sense of splendid isolation here, aided by the house being hidden down a precipitous slope, 200 m (656 ft) from the nearest road. Big windows frame the views over the bay, allowing the owners to observe the fleets of little white boats from their vantage point.

There is a distinct sense of the theatrical about the vast interior, carefully refurbished by its current owner who bought the run-down house for less than its land value in 1993. Most of the changes simply upgraded the 1960s materials with higher-specification modern equivalents, such as the blue-tinted and

SPACESHIP HOUSE

Left: On its outward side the structure touches lightly on the cliff face, windows facing downward to take in the views. A cantilevered concrete balcony runs around the circumference of the house allowing the owners to literally walk out and touch the treetops.

Right: The fleet of little white sailing boats in the bay below seem blissfully unaware that their very move is being observed by the many-eyed white disc hovering above.

ARCHITECT	Eugene Van Grecken
LOCATION	Bayview, Sydney, Australia
CREATED	1963

laminated windows for the lower floor and new 25 mm (¹/₂ in.) thick glass for the fourteen circular skylights that puncture the domed roof. The new glass provides for peace of mind when the house is being buffeted by the occasion storm and reduces solar gain to keep internal temperatures in check. The interior is split over two levels, which, thanks to the self-supporting span of the dome, are entirely open plan. Rooms are created by dividers and light stud walls, the most dramatic of which curves around to form the main dining area. Its original chrome plastic bubble tiles add that Barbarella-esque sense of retro 1960s funk to an interior that had spent the previous decade being hired out for bachelor parties. Perhaps the most cinematic of all the features, is the kidney-shaped, slate-topped coffee table that swivels back to reveal a secret spiral staircase to the floor below. Touches like these give the interior a heightened sense of unreality, as though the occupants are living on a Ken Adam set for a James Bond film. The stairs descend past the jutting sandstone of the cliffs, which has been allowed to form the inner wall, before opening out onto the lip of the concrete slab that forms the perimeter balcony. Resting on its wooden handrail, visitors find themselves floating above the bay as the ground falls sharply away.

At once dramatically modern, but somehow sympathetic to its surroundings, the Spaceship is the embodiment of the optimistic architecture that we once thought the future would hold.

Film-inspired touches, such as the hidden staircase under the swivelling kidney-shaped coffee table, all contribute to the feeling of walking into Blofeld's lair.

Below: On the lower floor the natural sandstone cliff projects into the living space. This technique is also employed in many John Lautner houses and blurs the distinction between inside and out.

Right: Two rings of circular skylights act like natural spotlights, flooding the open interior with light. The circular table could equally be the setting for a quiet romantic meal for two, or a high-powered conference to decide the future of SPECTRE.

ARCHITECT	Cesar Pelli & Associates
LOCATION	Kuala Lumpur, Malaysia
CREATED	1992–97

PETRONAS TOWERS

The skyscraper is arguably America's greatest contribution to the history of architecture, being one of the few building types to originate entirely from those shores. It was the demand by large financial institutions and industrial corporations for headquarters and office space, coupled with the limited land available that gave architects rising ambitions. Driven by the same market forces, New York and Chicago developed a healthy rivalry that ensured that heights just kept rising. The emerging steel-frame technology drove the race to new heights until, just forty years after Chicago's brick-walled Monadnock Building topped out at 66 m (217 ft), the silver Empire State Building was piercing the clouds over New York at 381 m (1252 ft), becoming an overnight symbol of American commercial clout. But what began as a local derby between these US commercial centres has now shifted to the other side of the world, where the economic giants of the Far East are locked in a familiar struggle to support the tallest skyscrapers, each striving to outdo the rest. In 1997 it was the twin spires of the Petronas Towers in Malaysia that finally wrested the coveted title of 'tallest building in the world' from the West, soaring a dizzying 452 m (1483 ft) above the Golden Triangle of the Federal capital, Kuala Lumpur.

In contrast to its title-stripping nemesis, Taipei 101 (2004), the Petronas Towers' underlying frame is entirely made of structural concrete, rather than concrete-filled steel sections, as Malaysian contractors were more experienced in this type of construction. The tapering columns, 2.4 m (8 ft) in diameter at their base, are linked by arched ring beams in the same material. The whole building rests on a cast concrete raft 4.5 m (15 ft) thick, which is stabilized by 104 barbette piles extending to depths of 45 to 105 m (148 to 344 ft). All of this concrete mass is hidden behind a glittering façade of stainless steel and green-tinted glass that catches the lingering rays of the tropical sunsets.

Left: The sky bridge, with its V-shaped supports, connects the viewing decks on the forty-first and forty-second floors and turns the two towers into a single symbolic gateway.

Right: Compared to the blocky forms that have dominated high-rise design in the West, the Petronas towers offer that exhilarating element of 'Flash Gordon' fantasy that the Chrysler Building first brought to the genre when its glittering spire was unveiled in 1930.

One of the most striking features of the design is the two-storey 'sky-bridge' that connects the towers at the forty-first and forty-second floors, allowing workers to commute between the two buildings. The bridge posed a particular set of problems for the engineers as it needed to accommodate movement in both towers, which might not necessarily be uniform or even in the same direction. Their solution was to support its 750 tonne (827 ton) weight on two V-shaped three-pin arches whose ends terminate in spherical bearings resting on 'knuckles' positioned at the twenty-ninth floor. These rotational pins, effectively giant ball-and-socket joints, provide a wider range of movement than could have been achieved with ridged junctions. The 58.4 m (192 ft) long bridge was assembled and shipped to site in five sections; the two legs, two end pieces and the main bridge. These were installed in that sequence, with the legs being pinned to the sides of the towers until the middle section was in place, and then swung into position to be connected.

Ironically, the competition to build this triumphal gateway to a new Malaysia was won by an American practice, Cesar Pelli & Associates, which was already well established in the high-rise world for having designed London's Canary Wharf Tower (1986). Rather than simply transplanting Anglo-American skyscraper style to the Far East, the architects' winning design found inspiration in the art forms of Islam, the dominant religion in Malaysia. In cross-section, the tower is based on two interlocking squares, one rotated at forty-five degrees to the other to form an eight-point star, a motif found throughout the Islamic world in carved screens, ceramics and metalwork. The insertion of small circular infills between the square edges contribute to the building's visual interest, alternating sharp angle against curved surface, while the glittering stainless-steel floors step back at six intervals and culminate in spires that glow in the night, like pulsing antenna.

Just as Jean Nouvel did with his highly acclaimed Arab Institute in Paris (1988), Cesar Pelli has demonstrated that the elegant geometry developed by a religion forbidden the use of figurative elements in decoration, is a visual language capable of being translated into striking modern architecture on a monumental scale. Kuala Lumpur's twin towers are symbolic, not only of Malaysia's high economic aspirations, but also of its underlying cultural roots.

Left: Viewed at night, the rings of the step-backs glow like power level indicators, giving them the appearance of futuristic electric pylons or mooring masts for some vast spacecraft.

Right: While the building owes its cross-section to Islamic art, the uppermost staggered layers and spires seem to make reference to the Buddhist pagodas that are found on the Malaysian peninsula near its border with Thailand.

HIGH DESERT HOUSE

A distant planet's surface can be even more hostile to the intergalactic traveller than the cold depths of space itself, but there is one architect who would thrive however hostile an environment he found himself in. Faced with a seemingly desolate arena, Kendrick Bangs Kellogg's design for the High Desert House did not require the arid, boulder-strewn site to be cleared. Instead he made a comprehensive survey of the area's topography, and inserted the concrete forms of the house among the jostling boulders in order to make the least physical impact upon the landscape. This project certainly embodies his mantra that 'the more challenging the terrain, the better the architecture.'[2]

Built for two successful graphic artists and their son, the house was an ongoing labour of love for architect Kellogg and artisan John Vugrin for over fifteen years, the design slowly evolving as new possibilities presented themselves. But their

Left: A house at one with its setting. From a distance the interlocking leaves blend seamlessly with the surrounding rocks.

Below: Emerging from the shadowy interior, the residents can sit by the pebble-edged pool under the canopy of the armadillo's scales.

ARCHITECT	Kendrick Bangs Kellogg
LOCATION	Palm Springs, California, USA
CREATED	1989–2003

The house flows down the hillside, with the twenty-six overlapping concrete leaves forming a rough herringbone pattern to create the basic shell.

clients' patience paid off as this careful partnership created a true twenty-first-century 'gesamtkunstwerk', literally, 'a total work of art'. The powerful sculptural form is sited in a landscape shaped by even more powerful natural forces. Kellogg, conscious of the house's proximity to the San Andreas Fault, devised an ingenious structure in which each of the twenty-six concrete 'leaves' forming the shell of the building are capable of moving independently. In the event of an earthquake, the columns, rooted 2 m (7 ft) into the natural rock, would gently sway, absorbing the force of the tremors. Between each leaf, the tempered glass of the windows is set in rubberised gaskets that are able to accommodate the movements caused by aftershocks, and could be easily replaced should they ever be fractured by a major earthquake.

This bespoke home is evidence of Kellogg's career-long battle for reduced energy consumption – most notable during his tenure as Commissioner of Housing and Community Development for the State of California. The sheer size and mass of the concrete helps maintain an even temperature in the house, with the dense leaves slowly absorbing the sun's rays by day and then radiating heat after dark. Leaving the doors open at night allows the building to cool, so that it is ready to begin the cycle again by morning.

Leaving the glaring desert sun behind (temperatures here regularly reach 120°F or 49°C in the shade), the visitor climbs a broad flight of stone steps and enters the shadowy lair. There is a sense of being swallowed whole by some fantastic prehistoric beast that is slowly turning itself inside out, its hard metallic tail somehow spiralling inside its belly. The 'dragon's tail', as many visitors have called it, is constructed from 2.5 cm (1 in.) thick steel plates, spaced like vertebrae along a spine of carefully rusted steel. Along its length are the glass-topped workstations at which the owners produce their graphic art.

Every aspect of the house has been crafted by hand, from the bathroom mosaic of pebbles gathered from the desert floor to the bronze doorframes and copper chimney flue. Kellogg is a 'hands-on' architect, and would often bend iron-reinforcing bars over his knee to describe shapes to the client. Once approved, such bars were instantly welded to create the skeleton to which the concrete was applied.

The High Desert House puts form before function, but not at the latter's expense, proving that even handcrafted one-offs can have enviable sustainable credentials. This controlled metamorphosis of modern materials into living fossil is both ancient and modern, and one that could easily belong to a galaxy far, far away.

The house has no internal walls, instead boulders act as natural room dividers for the more private spaces. The main living area is dominated by the whiplash tendril of the rusted steel spine of the desk that curls through the house.

Above: Attention to detail holds every element of this house together; electrical sockets are disguised seamlessly behind enamelled hinged brass covers.

Left: John Vugrin crafted individual bronze frames and locks for every door in the house, all with the aesthetic of prehistoric bones. The two doors leading to the stone deck were sandblasted to such a depth that the patterns seem almost three-dimensional.

The work of Santiago Calatrava is not easily classified, being an almost unique blend of architecture, engineering and sculpture. Whatever the function of the building, the client can be assured that the architect will deliver a showstopper, an instantly photogenic icon and one that will generate worldwide interest in their town or city. Whereas Calatrava is usually called upon to produce a single flamboyant focal point for new activity, his home city of Valencia gave him the scope to create a whole new world.

A vast complex of buildings, the City of Arts and Sciences looks, at first glance, to be a monumental sculpture park, or perhaps a prehistoric graveyard, featuring the sun-bleached ribcages of a long extinct species. The setting itself could hardly be more dramatic. Following a disastrous flood in 1957, the river Turia was diverted along a canal to the south of the city. This left a 7 km (4.4 miles) channel of dried riverbed, midway between the old city of Valencia and the coastal district of Nazaret. Parts of this strip were planted in the 1960s to become an elegant promenade through the city centre with views out to sea. But in the early 1990s, moves were made to develop the remaining site along more dynamic lines and Calatrava was chosen to mastermind the scheme. Starting with two streamlined new bridges that span the promenade, he began to add a series of buildings that slowly filled the 350,000 m^2 (3.8 million sq. ft) site, culminating in 2006 with the Reina Sofia Palau de les Artes (Palace of the Arts).

The complex is based around four principal buildings: the Palau de las Artes, L'Hemisfèric (Planetarium), the Science Museum Principe Felipe (Science Museum) and the L'Umbracle. The latter must be a strong contender for the most elaborate promenade-cum-carpark in history, with a magnificent glazed arched roof that soars over the pathway to form an elongated palm house. Calatrava's trademark cast-concrete components

CITY OF ARTS AND SCIENCES

The elegant conical forms with their crazed tiled surfaces are the roofs to the spiralling staircases that lead visitors down into the subterranean car parks.

ARCHITECT	Santiago Calatrava
LOCATION	Valencia, Spain
CREATED	1991–2006

are here softened by the Gaudíesque use of fragments of shattered ceramic tiles (still an important industry in Valencia) that coat their bone-like forms. Water plays a large part in the landscaping, Calatrava having effectively reinstated the river with a continuous flow of stunning architectural monuments basking in reflecting pools. Covering large areas, these pools extend right up against the buildings and mirror their surroundings. Concourses provide direct axial links between the structures. The floors to these concourses are sometimes glass, partly floodlit, allowing visitors to see the water beneath. But it is at night that the buildings are at their most magical, when underwater floodlights, distorted by the rippling water, send sinuous waves of light washing over the smooth concrete bones of the sleeping giants.

Calatrava's extensive experience of designing stations clearly informs this expansive work. Stations are transitory spaces open to a public that is free to circulate throughout, with access to the platforms being restricted only to ticket holders. Stations are required to advertise their presence, welcome beacons to travellers, as with Calatrava's exemplary TGV Station in Lyons (1994, see pp 104–07). These same qualities can be found in the Valencia complex, where the architectural promenade encourages casual passers-by to stroll among the buildings, without requiring them to pay for entry. The promenade incorporates open public spaces that permit pedestrians to partially experience the building interiors, much as Norman Foster's Great Court draws people into the British Museum by creating a covered thoroughfare that people use as an alternative route.

Whatever future flourishes Calatrava has up his sleeve, the City of Arts and Sciences is likely to remain his most complete work, a wide canvas on which he has created an almost unrestrained exercise in the architecture of cultural tourism that has reinvented this coastal town as a twenty-first-century city.

The north-facing atrium of the Science Museum clearly demonstrates Calatrava's lightness of touch. The soaring 'ribcage' of the delicate frame, some 40 m (131 feet) high, is typical of his references to skeletal, biomorphic forms.

The southern elevation of the Science Museum is a more complex affair, with a diamond pattern of interlocking ribs that extend outwards to form brackets that support a dramatic elevated gangway. Accessed from either end by triangulated bridges, this gangway forms the principle means of entering the museum.

The stately sequence of buildings appears like a futuristic fleet of ships sailing in an orderly line down the shallow river that Calatrava has so carefully created (left to right: the Palace of the Arts, the Planetarium and the Science Museum).

Overleaf: The Planetarium takes on the menacing guise of a scarab beetle half submerged in the lake, glaring at visitors approaching along the causeway. The auditorium's shell is made from laminated glass and aluminium with sections that can open to the sky.

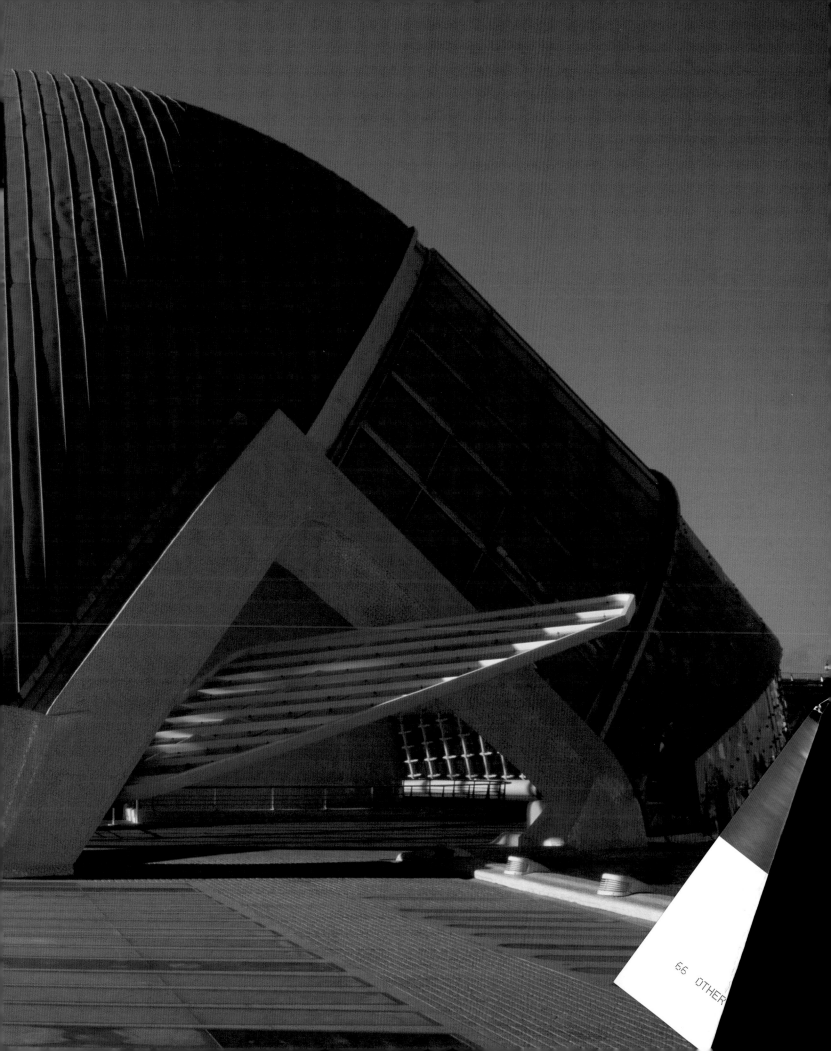

The Netherlands has a long history of imaginative modern architecture stretching back through the twentieth century and including such notable icons as Gerrit Rietveld's revolutionary Schröder House of 1924. This physical realization of the strong rectilinear lines of a Mondrian canvas now feels quite austere compared to current Dutch tastes for extreme architecture, which are perhaps more in line with the crystalline-inspired forms of Michel de Klerk and the work of the Amsterdam School. De Klerk's masterpiece, the triangular social housing block Het Scheep (The Ship), is a dizzying array of patterned brick complete with a mast-like spire and protruding organic pod windows. Built in 1921, just three years before the controlled refinement of Schröder House, it stands in the district of Spaarndammerbuurt just north-west of the central station. But if a visitor to Amsterdam leaves the nineteenth-century Dutch Renaissance station behind, and chooses instead to head south-east, they will soon find themselves standing on the edge of the old Oosterdok looking at a 'ship' of a very different era.

On a peninsula jutting into the Oosterdok, is the looming prow of Renzo Piano's NEMO, the National Centre for Science and Technology, which is part of the ongoing programme of renewal for this dockyard in decline. Inspired by the many ships that used

NEMO (NATIONAL CENTRE FOR SCIENCE & TECHNOLOGY)

Left: The building takes on its most futuristic aspect at night when washed with light from below. The footbridge enables visitors to access the building from both sides of the dock.

Right: Visitors approaching the roof terrace from the rear must climb a ramp whose brick wedge support ends before it can touch the building, giving the impression that people are boarding a giant vessel from a gangway, prior to embarking for the unknown.

ARCHITECT	Renzo Piano Building Workshop
LOCATION	Amsterdam, the Netherlands
CREATED	1992–97

these sheltered waters, Piano has created a distinctive maritime form akin to the bows of a vast liner, ploughing its way towards the channel to the open sea. The bows form the front of a long wedge that tails back to meet a ramp rising from the dockside. The form belongs to the harbour, rather than the city, and appears at a distance to be temporarily moored prior to departure, sitting on its largely underwater piles.

The attraction's popular name, NEMO (meaning literally 'nobody'), has strong associations with the worlds of adventure and fantasy, being shared with the Captain of the Nautilus in Jules Verne's 1869 novel '20,000 Leagues Under the Sea'. The connotations seem perfectly apt given the maritime context and the exploratory nature of the exhibits, with the whirling wheels and fans of the installations giving the interior the appearance of a futuristic engine room preparing to propel the giant craft down into the depths below. The exterior is almost completely clad in pre-oxidized copper panels; beautifully folded and detailed in much the same way as the lead sheet roofs of Piano's later Rome Auditorium, (1997–2004). The copper panels have weathered sympathetically to a distinctive green, making the building stand out against its mainly concrete surroundings. The material also makes a further reference to the local shipbuilding industry, as seventeenth- and eighteenth-century Dutch merchantmen, in common with many ships of the period, had their wooden hulls sheathed in copper in order to protect them from burrowing crustaceans.

Piano believed NEMO was an opportunity to provide Amsterdam with a raised space from which visitors could view the city, which is unusual among European capitals for being almost totally flat and lacking in natural vantage points. The access ramp from the wharf on Prins Hendrikkade takes visitors up onto the sloping roof of the building, which the architects have turned into a continuous flight of wide concrete steps interrupted by the terrace of a rooftop restaurant. In the summer the area is transformed into an artificial beach so that Amsterdammers can catch a few rays while gazing out over their city.

NEMO proves that landmark buildings need not be demanding narcissistic icons, but can take visual cues from their surroundings to provide a city with a profitable tourist attraction and, simultaneously, a new outlook on itself.

The sharply inclined bows jut out into the docks, supported by extensive underwater piling. The dramatic sloping of the roof means that visitors who climb all the way to the top find themselves 30 m (98 ft) above the water.

The banked rows of steps and roof terrace restaurant provide visitors and locals alike with the opportunity to relax and gaze over Amsterdam from this manmade vantage point.

The interior is an Aladdin's cave with a
dense mix of whirring fans and spinning
wheels to excite children's interest
and to convey the underlying scientific
principles behind the everyday
phenomena of electricity, magnetism,
light and colour.

Spain is home to some of the world's most exciting and sculptural modern architecture, from Calatrava's City of Arts and Sciences in Valencia, to Frank Gehry's seminal Guggenheim in Bilbao, but there are some less publicized gems tucked away in its provinces. Cáceres sits quietly on the river Algars in western Spain, its surroundings beautified by well-preserved Roman and Moorish ruins, giving it that timeless quality beloved by tourists. But in 2003 the impressive, Romanesque-Gothic diaphragm arches of its church of Santa Ana were spectacularly upstaged when the town acquired a fresh set of curves in its new bus station.

The bus station is a deliberately playful sculpture, designed to excite the children who play in the nursery and school on either side of the plot. Its basic form is that of a continuous concrete ribbon folded over to enclose a waiting room and provide a canopy protecting passengers from the glare of the sun. To give space to this expressive form, Justo García Rubio chose to put the café and travel agent's store in a subterranean basement, leaving just the waiting room and canopy showing above the surface. Though a twenty-first-century building, the bus station has a satisfying handcrafted appearance that has been supplied by the impressions in the concrete of the grain and edge of every plank of the wooden shuttering. This gives a much richer effect than the complex steel formwork used to produce Calatrava's colder, seamless polished surfaces. The structure's texture harks back to that icon of postwar design, Eero Saarinen's TWA terminal at JFK Airport, New York (1956–62), with which it shares its rippling surface, like a baulk of timber that has been cut with a Bronze Age adze, rather than a steel-bladed plane.

This sense of craftsmanship, of an object bearing its maker's mark, plays a key role in Spanish architecture and can be found in the work of Antonio Gaudí, with his organic, mosaic-clad Parc Güell and the concrete accretions of the Sagrada Familia in Barcelona. With the Casar de Cáceres bus station, García has given his home town a modest building, but one that can be shared by the nation, adding another timeless classic to Spanish architecture.

CASAR DE CACERES BUS STATION

Above: Two curving white concrete panels create the overall form. The larger of the two, 740 m (2,428 ft) long, forms the canopy that soars over incoming buses, while the smaller 380 m (1,247 ft) length rings the waiting room.

Left: The strong evening light picks up each seam and exposed aggregate, transforming the undulating curves into a ribbon of coarsely woven fabric, draped over the elliptical glass box of the café.

ARCHITECT	Justo García Rubio
LOCATION	Casar de Cáceres, Extremadura Region, Spain
CREATED	2003

Bart Prince is an architect capable of creating fantasy homes that would not seem out of place in a Tolkeinesque landscape or a Jules Verne novel, but it would erroneous to label his work as that of pure fiction. Prince prefers to think of his style as both rational and organic, embracing all the lessons nature has to offer, but being in no way a slavish imitation. In the Sun Valley House, he seems to have created a landscape in miniature, with its undulating curves rising like little hills out of the valley floor. But a dissection of his design process reveals a building that is reacting to, rather than replicating, its environment. After all, to try and build a house that could compete with this rugged landscape would be madness, the craggy ranges and golden plains being simply too vast a canvas for even the boldest gesture to have any impact.

In plan, the house ripples in waves, with four interlocking volumes facing first one way then the other, forming a chain of rooms through which a central spinal corridor is threaded. The layout is a direct response to the client's need for both guest and master suites to have some degree of privacy and separation, but still remain linked to the main living spaces. As the expansive site did not require a compact design, Prince's solution was to provide two wings, facing in opposite directions, and backed by high curving walls of split-faced concrete blocks. This manmade material was chosen in preference to natural stone as it allowed the walls to have a slimmer profile, as well as a consistent integral colour and texture. The blocks were custom-made in Salt Lake City and have moulded internal cavities that improve their insulation properties and allow additional reinforcement to be inserted.

Below: The two wings of the house allow guests and residents a degree of privacy, while giving every room uninterrupted views of the dramatic landscape.

Right: The master and guest rooms are linked to the central spaces by means of projecting galleries, supported on red oxidised steel hoops and clad in fir planks and shingles like defensive medieval hoardings.

SUN VALLEY HOUSE

ARCHITECT	Bart Prince
LOCATION	Idaho, USA
CREATED	1989–91

Visitors enter at the centre of the chain, coming into the main living room with its wall-hugging built-in seating. The overhead fir beams cast zebra-stripe shadows across the white upholstery.

The concrete foundations raise the house above the ground, anticipating the heavy snowfalls that form a blanket covering up to 1.2 m (4 ft) thick, and allowing guests and residents to enjoy separate uninterrupted views of the pristine winter landscape, even in the coldest months. In late summer the waving, waist-high grasses rise to a similar height as the snows, blending with the warm rich colour of the split-face block walls to blur the line between house and hill still further. The curving roofs are covered in shingles that have naturally weathered from a rusty brown to a silvery grey. To make the most of the often adverse weather conditions, Prince designed them as 'cold roofs', with an air space between the outer shingles and the inner structure. This prevents the warmth of the house from melting the snow that settles on the roof, allowing it to act as a further layer of insulation rather than running off to form dangerously large icicles. The steep pitch and curved walls provide the strength to support the additional weight and help deflect the strong icy winds that blow down the valley.

The use of the manmade blocks allowed the forms to be realized, but the enduring impression is that of warm shingles and beams, of natural materials sculpted into supernatural forms. Prince is not forcing the building's functions into preconceived shapes, but is simply responding to the client's brief in his own unique way, providing an organic solution within the cost constraints. Amazingly, this holiday home was intended to be sold at a later date, which accounts for the less bespoke nature of the fittings compared to those of Prince's earlier Price House. Even under new ownership, the Sun Valley house remains a fine example of how an architect can respond to both client and climate to create a house that is at one with its surroundings.

The twisting geometry of the copper-clad skylights, which form the vertebrae of the main roof section, finishes at each end with cylindrical towers with domed skylights that house guest toilets and a laundry room.

TAIPEI 101

In the Far East, where the 'Tiger' economies predominate, size is undeniably important. Taiwan received a welcome boost to its reputation on 31 December 2004, when Taipei 101 was officially declared the tallest building in the world, measuring in at 508 m (1,667 ft). Topping its Malaysian rival, the twin Petronas Towers, by a comfortable 56 m (184 ft), Taipei 101 tower boasts the world's fastest elevators – double-deckers capable of whisking passengers up to the eighty-ninth floor in just 39 seconds. Above the eighty-ninth floor a further twelve levels bring the total floors to the magic 101 that gives the building its name.

Architects C. Y. Lee liken the form to that of the native bamboo shoot and flower, though there are other references to Chinese architectural elements, such as pagodas. The main 'trunk' of the tower is comprised of eight identical modules (eight stands for 'blooming' or 'success' and is considered a lucky number in Taiwan), on top of which come eleven stepped mechanical equipment levels, topped by a 60 m (197 ft) pinnacle. Each module is separated by fire barriers that function in the same way as watertight compartments in a ship, containing and limiting any damage to the main structure. The seven-degree outward slope of the modules' double-layered glass faces allows for better downward views, and reduces the solar glare to the interior. The base or 'root' of the tower, some twenty-six floors high, tapers in at five degrees from a footprint roughly 53 m (174 ft) square. The first five floors contain the shopping mall, with its impressively ornate atrium ceiling depicting a vision of the future worthy of H. G. Wells.

The building's strength lies in the use of 'megacolumns', a concept brought to the Taipei project in 1998 by New York City–based engineers Thornton-Tomasetti, and originally

Left: The fusion of ancient Chinese forms and modern construction methods, combining cooling fin mouldings with quatrefoil connectors, gives the ceiling of the five-storey shopping mall a strange, almost Victorian Gothic appearance.

Right: At night the tower's staggered storeys are edged with light as though a gambler has hit the jackpot on some immense fruit machine. These ledges also provide the space for external fire safety decks, packed with firefighting, smoke displacement and communications equipment.

ARCHITECT	C. Y. Lee & Partners
LOCATION	Taipei, Taiwan
CREATED	1998–2004

eveloped by them some ten years earlier for the unrealized iglin Beitler Tower, Chicago. Together with Taiwan firm vergreen Consulting Engineering, Thornton-Tomasetti created n underlying structure that begins on each face of the building ith two 'megacolumns' running up either side of the centre line. hese columns have a cross-section of 3 x 2.4 m (10 x 8 ft) and are onstructed from welded steel up to 8 cm (3 in.) thick. Erected in ections up to the level of the sixty-second floor, the hollow olumns were then pumped full of concrete at a pressure of 0,000 psi. From the sixty-second floor the structure is entirely ade of steel in order to reduce weight and prevent the building om becoming top heavy. The scale of these component parts ontributes to the tower's colossal overall weight (estimated at 00,000 tonnes, 771,619 tons), which is raising concerns in some uarters that it may actually be placing too much stress on the arth's crust, making earthquakes more likely.

To give peace of mind to the 12,000 people who can potentially ork and shop here, the tower's designers have gone to xtraordinary lengths to allow for the unstable tectonics of the egion. The need for such measures was tragically reinforced on 1 May 2002, when five construction workers were killed by two cranes falling from the fifty-sixth floor following an earthquake measuring 6.8 on the Richter scale. The engineers' solution provides a series of massive dampeners throughout the building; the most obvious of which takes the form of a giant steel ball suspended from steel cables in a cradle opposite the mezzanine restaurants on the eighty-seventh floor. A pin, some 60 cm (2 ft) thick, projects from the base of the ball and passes through a steel ring that is attached to four hydraulic pistons that limit the movement of the pin to around 1 m (3.3 ft). Any movement of the building causes the ball to swing like a pendulum, pressing the pin against the wall of the ring, and the pistons absorb the energy. With this giant pendulum, the designers seem to be seeking to reassure diners that Taipei 101 really is here to stay, perhaps encouraging them to stay for dessert.

The controversy about the long-term implications of building such massively heavy skyscrapers continues, but other cities in Asia (including Delhi and Shanghai) have their own plans for even more gigantic towers, quietly whirring their way through banks of engineering software. It can only be a matter of time before the imaginative bamboo shoot of Taipei 101 is outgrown by its rivals, and so the race to be the tallest building in the world continues.

eft: The large ball that forms the tuned ass dampener can be viewed by sitors on the mezzanine level of the ghty-seventh floor, two floors below e public viewing gallery.

ight: The 6 m (20 ft) diameter ball the tuned mass dampener was sembled on-site from layers of steel 2.5 cm (approx. 5 in.) thick, welded to a adle suspended by four sets of cables d weighs in at 660 tonnes (730 tons), a cost in excess of £439,000.

BRION CEMETERY

Carlo Scarpa's body of work is not what you would immediately describe as overtly futuristic. The path he trod was a distinctive but careful one, his speciality being the sensitive conversion of older buildings into exhibition spaces without resorting to pastiche. The line between his interventions and the original structures never blurs, but somehow marry perfectly.

His masterpieces include the Regional Gallery of Sicily, Palermo (housed in the fifteenth-century Palazzo Abatellis), the Museo di Castelvecchio (within a fourteenth-century fortified manor) and the Canova Sculpture Museum in Passagno. His final great work was a family cemetery commissioned by Onorina Brion shortly after the death of her husband Giuseppe Brion in September 1968. The site chosen was Giuseppe's birth place, the small town of San Vito d'Altivole. As co-founders of the progressive electronics firm Brion-Vega, the Brion family could afford grand funereal arrangements and they purchased an L-shaped plot of land running around the edge of the local cemetery that looked out over the farmland beyond.

With this site, Scarpa was free to use his own visual language to create a small parallel world, producing a truly modern interpretation of a place of rest. Eschewing the classical columns and porticos traditionally employed in Italian cemeteries, Scarpa went further back in time, to the mass and solidity of Ancient Egypt, the gently sloping pyramids of which seem to be echoed in Brion's outer walls. There are also hints of the Mayan civilization that influenced Frank Lloyd Wright, whom Scarpa so admired.

ARCHITECT	Carlo Scarpa
LOCATION	San Vito d'Altivole, Treviso, Italy
CREATED	1969–78

Right: Seated in the water pavilion, visitors gaze out over the lily pond and its raised square with outstretched arms that echo the stretched form of the arcosolium beyond. The channel running down the side of the propylaeum takes water to the arched canopy over the sarcophagi, symbolically suggestive of life slowly ebbing away.

Below: 'Arcosolium' is a Latin term from early Christian times used to describe the niches in the catacombs where important person or martyrs were interred. The stepped circular pools are fed by a narrow concrete channel running from the lily pond surrounding the water pavilion.

The underlying geometry was ancient, but the detailing was new, with the result that this modern burial ground has a sense of history much greater than its true age while still belonging to the twentieth century. In this garden of the dead, the structures rest like the ruins of an ancient, yet advanced, civilization, long abandoned at the outskirts of this quiet Italian town.

Scarpa encircled the plot with a leaning concrete rampart, providing the inner space with a sense of privacy. The three main elements – a pavilion, the Brion's own tomb and a chapel – are sited in the corners of the L-shaped plot and carefully linked by paths and sightlines. Most important of all is the canopy that arches over the couple's sarcophagi which Scarpa referred to as an 'arcosolium'. The sarcophagi themselves have white marble bases and black stone tops, both heavily carved with Scarpa's distinctive stepped reliefs. Foliage trails over the edges of the arch, softening the points where it touches the ground.

Standing in a lily pond at the southernmost tip of the site, the pavilion plays host to the living, who can sit and contemplate the movement of water as it travels down a narrow channel to the arched arcosolium where the departed rest. This could be a subtle

reference to the Egyptian belief that spirits crossed the Nile to get to the underworld, the river that sustained them through life transporting them in death. Yet this is not a morbid place, but one that Scarpa chose to keep as open as possible in order to create a civic garden where the townsfolk can sit and meditate in the fresh air. No element that is ordinary is allowed to permeate the space, giving the visitor the sense that they have left the modern world behind. The attention to detail, down to the polished steel door hinges and inlaid glass tiles, makes the whole experience memorable. Scarpa was obsessed with craft, visiting the workshops to see his designs being made and forming personal relationships with the craftsmen.

The cemetery is evidence that an architect who sees the underlying spiritual essence in past styles can return to the present with principles to apply, rather than motifs to reproduce. Modern production designers simply raid history and bring back seemingly random architectural elements to merge with what they purport to be 'visions' of the future, but are in fact a rehash of the past. But Scarpa immersed himself in the spirituality of a culture that was preoccupied with the afterlife and, in so doing, tapped a far richer seam of inspiration. His cemetery at Brion is no plaster filmset but a concrete reality, modern materials gently weathered over time to almost ancient effect. It is fitting that Scarpa is also buried here, able to enjoy the tranquillity he so carefully created.

The submerged algae-covered ridges of the slabs supporting the water pavilion's base contrast with the still white concrete of those above the surface. The spliced Cor-ten steel columns that support the canopy meet the concrete base in exquisitely designed brass interlocking junctions.

Right: Cast back-to-back, Scarpa's repeated ziggurat mouldings appropriately form a cross, directly aligned between the two sarcophagi, and marking the end of the channel drawn from the lily pond.

Reflections in the still water multiply the lines of the carefully moulded concrete ziggurat decoration that connects so many elements in Scarpa's design. This overgrown V-shaped section marks the beginning of the higher wall that forms the secluded backdrop to the water pavilion.

Whenever the topic of the new Scottish Parliament is raised, it is never long before conversation turns to money, but then money was always at the heart of the debate about Scotland's independence. The loss of its autonomy was rubber-stamped by the Act of Union in 1707, and brought about by the failure of the speculative Darien Scheme in Panama that wiped out 25 per cent of Scotland's liquid assets and plunged it into crisis. The promise of compensation from the English (£400,000, to be precise) overcame any reservations the Scottish aristocracy might have had about this constitutional capitulation and, together with deliberate English trade embargoes on Scottish goods, helped bring the treaty into being. Scotland's Parliament was dissolved, seemingly forever. It is perhaps with a touch of irony that when the Scottish Parliament re-emerged through the process of devolved government in 1999, it then came to be housed in a building that cost the joint exchequer so dearly. Finished three years late and, at £420 million, some £370 million over budget, from an historical perspective, it might appear to have been cheaper to buy the country in the first place, than to provide it with a new seat of government.

The tale of the Scottish Parliament building is touched by human tragedy, with both the client, Scotland's first elected

SCOTTISH PARLIAMENT

Left: At night the leaf-like skylight looks like the menacing cockpit covers on a dispersing squadron of star-fighters. Behind them rise the towers of the meeting rooms and second debating chamber, covered in abstract steel and concrete motifs.

Right: The language of the building includes cathedral-like buttresses beautifully cast in concrete, which project from the walls of the debating chamber to support the complex ceiling web.

ARCHITECT	EMBT Architectes & RMJM
LOCATION	Holyrood, Edinburgh, Scotland
CREATED	1998–2004

Top: The garden foyer is dominated by the swooping curved steel 'eyelids' of the leaf-shaped skylights, that directly refer to the folded leaves Miralles presented to the competition jury.

Bottom: The elliptical debating chamber forms the heart of the building with its ceiling a forest of steel tension rods and timber compression beams seated in complex steel connecting nodes; all part of the detailing that absorbed so much of the budget.

Minister Donald Dewar, and the Spanish architect, Enric Miralles, dying in 2000, some four years before the parliament was completed. Dewar had always campaigned for a new building to house Scotland's elected representatives, rather than a simple refurbishment of an existing structure. The competition he launched was won by Miralles, not with a completed scheme, but with a design proposal. The building was to represent the ancient Greek 'agora', an open public meeting place where people gathered to support the democratic ideal, and to form a physical representation of their union with the land that they governed. To the jury he presented a handful of bent stalks and folded leaves, which he proceeded to arrange into an organic diagram of a complex that seemed to flow out of the landscape. The jury was won over and unanimously supported the scheme.

It is these leaves and stalks that can be seen everywhere, woven into the fabric of the building from structural elements to surface pattern, part of the beautiful visual vocabulary that Miralles used to articulate this concept of a Parliament embodying the land itself. The richness of the interior is a symphony of natural and manmade materials, exquisite detailing and the finest craftsmanship. The stalks appear on bent oak window grills, concrete wall panels and even as steel microphone holders on the curving sycamore lecterns in the main debating chamber. What Miralles created was a land-scraping cathedral to the democratic age, constructed and fitted out with the same level of care as was lavished on the Palace of Westminster or Durham Cathedral. Yet the building deliberately eschews all notions of the dominance or pomp common to its historical precedents, opting instead to open its cluster of low-rise towers and foyers to the city at large, by hugging the landscape and flowing in several directions to present multiple busy faces and embrace grass-covered public arenas.

It remains to be seen whether the mountains of bad press that heralded its construction will blight the future of the building that sits in the shadow of the great rock of Arthur's seat, but the initial signs were promising. In the six months after its completion in 2004 the parliament became the most visited building in Scotland, with some 250,000 people being taken on specially conducted tours in a concerted attempt at reconciliation. Many appeared to leave converted, bewitched by Miralles's posthumous masterpiece. The architectural establishment also made its feelings known by awarding it the coveted Stirling Prize in 2005. It can only be hoped that the underlying concept of unity and openness that Miralles and Dewar both shared will win through in the end.

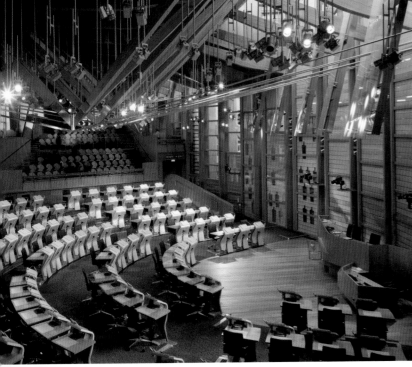

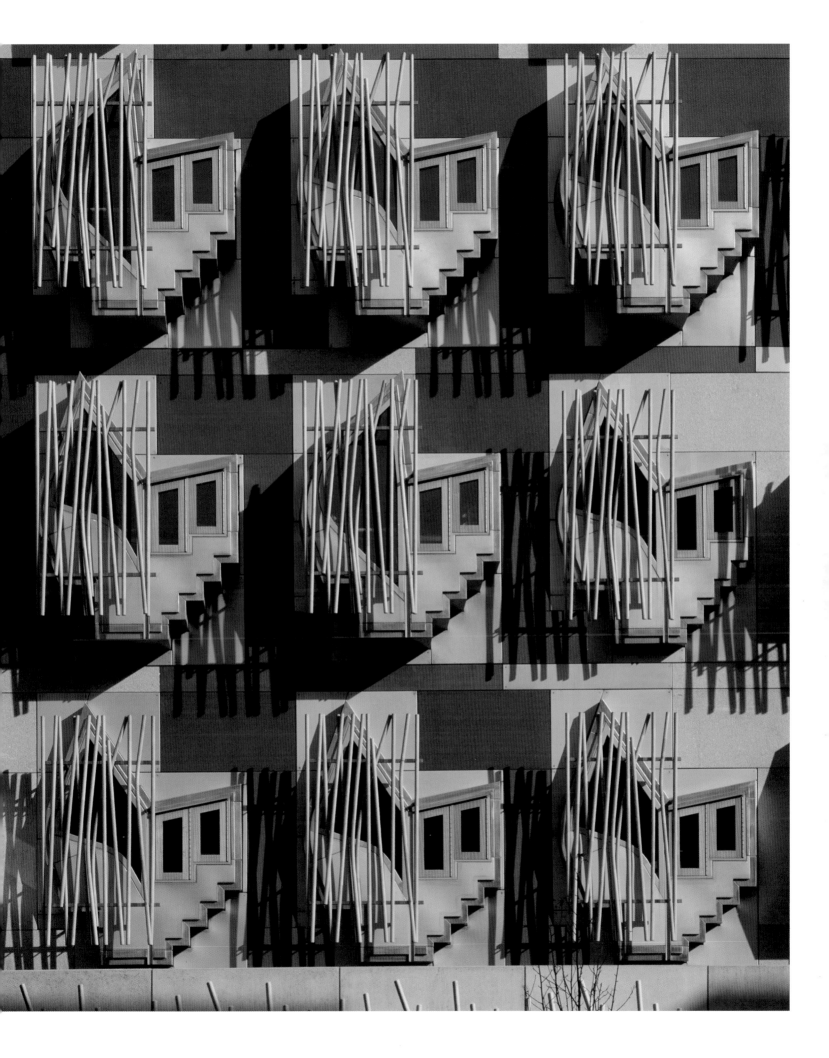

DEATH STARS AND TIE FIGHTERS

'If the world would only build temples to Machinery in the abstract then everything would be perfect.'

Percy Wyndham Lewis, English artist, 1882–1957

The Mechanical, the Manmade and the Menacing

The opening sequence to 'Star Wars: Episode IV' (1977) looms large in the collective cinematic memory. The hairs start to rise on the back of your neck as the massive steel underbelly of the Super Star Destroyer flies menacingly into view, seeming to glide straight over the audience's heads as it bears down on the tiny Rebel craft, like a giant metallic shark going in for the kill.

This was the defining image of science fiction for a whole cinema-going generation. A world dominated by advanced machines that could scatter mankind among the stars, whisking them from solar system to forest moon at light speed.

Yet, despite the promise of adventure and exploration that it offers, there is a pervading sense of disapproval for this reliance on technology, an undisguised disdain for the brutish functionality of the Laser Blaster and a reverence for the ethereal, glowing Light Sabre. 'An elegant weapon for a more civilized age', as the Jedi Obi-Wan Kenobi is heard to remark. It is as though the characters are secretly longing for a return to some past feudal era, an escape from the rapid mechanization of their world.

This is a theme as old as science-fiction cinema itself. From Fritz's Lang's oft-cited 'Metropolis' (1927) with its drone-like workers labouring over their steaming machines through to the evil Empire of 'Star Wars: Episode IV' (1977) enforcing its will with its squadrons of mass-produced TIE fighters, technology is almost synonymous with suppression, being portrayed as dark, gritty, unsympathetic, authoritarian and even Fascist. While supporters of the regime hide behind angular black masks, the free peoples are consistently associated with lighter tones and flowing organic curves, symbolic of their rebellious spirit.

Perhaps it was the scars left by the traumatic Industrial Revolution that caused so many film-makers to choose mechanistic environments as a visual shorthand for their apocalyptic visions. Yet many of the buildings in this chapter have been designed with the express purpose of revitalizing areas left deprived and desolate by the decline in heavy industry. They have adopted the nuts and bolts, girders and steel of their predecessors, but combined them with light and movement to become spaces for education, entertainment and even culture. Far from being uncompromising and sterile, they express their construction in informative ways, seducing us with glittering metal scales and halos of twinkling lights, to act as advertisements for man's mastery of science and technology.

The projects featured are all powerful expressions of the forces that brought them into being, with some absorbing the topography of their context. The Deep is at once both a tectonic wedge of geological history and a blunt-nosed supertanker balanced on the foreshore, at home on land or sea, while the graphic elements of the Vitra Fire Station create visual boundaries that help define the site it occupies. There are mechanical engines for both trade and transport, like Lloyd's of London, bearing its inner workings as it pumps power and air to hundreds of traders in an act of perpetual life support, and the Falkirk Wheel, transforming the act of lifting narrow boats into a work of kinetic sculpture.

The pursuit of spiritual and visual purity can be found in Hernández's poetic geometry based on the quadrants of a circle, while the Lowry Centre's jungle of distorted steel-clad geometric forms is an inspired composition of distinctive volumes designed to guide the first-time visitor through its warren of brightly coloured interiors. We even discover an organic undertone to the robotic edges of the Fuji Building in the Metabolist philosophy of creating buildings that imitate the cellular growth of our own skin.

With these buildings, architects have brought technology out of the shadows, and transported us willingly to a galaxy far, far away...

ARCHITECT	Richard Rogers Partnership
LOCATION	City of London, England
CREATED	1978–86

The two main elements of Rogers's design are shown side-by-side: the glazed barrel vault of the main atrium and one of the six service towers bristling with staircases and air-conditioning pipes and surmounted by the grey stack of plant rooms needed to power the building.

LLOYD'S OF LONDON

Lloyd's of London remains an icon of Thatcherite Britain, a cathedral to the power of London's money men and Richard Rogers's first major commission after his successful collaboration with Renzo Piano on the Centre Pompidou in Paris (1972–76). The shining steel staircases and exposed pipework were stunningly at odds with the pinstripe-suited tastes of its intended occupants. Finance was an industry unused to exposing itself to public scrutiny, and it suddenly found itself in a structure that exposed all its inner workings to the world.

The clarity of the plan is a continuation of themes explored at the Centre Pompidou, with the emphasis being a flexible, uncluttered layout capable of meeting the changing needs of its occupants. At Lloyd's, the design revolves around the main trading floor ('the Room') where the majority of insurance transactions occur. This being their third move in just fifty years, Lloyd's insisted that 'the Room' should be capable of operating throughout any future construction work in order to cause minimal disturbance to business should they need to expand. The basic structure comprises a rectangular block of up to twelve floors (partly linked by escalators), topped with a vaulted atrium and surrounded by a ring of six service towers, 95 m (312 ft) high. Rogers originally envisaged the towers as slender shafts of steel, like buttresses on a Gothic cathedral, or an entourage of turrets around a medieval keep. But as the design developed, it became clear that the additional heat generated by the increase in computers, and the anticipated rise in volumes of traders, would require a far more extensive air-conditioning system than originally planned. This led to the towers becoming more muscular and dominant, with large boxes on top to take the extra plant, giving the building its mechanistic character.

Left: The open sweep of 'the Room' takes up almost the entire ground floor, allowing the multitude of traders the face-to-face interaction they prefer.

Right: The drama of the highly textured façades is brought out at night by the dramatic lighting scheme designed by Gary Withers and his team at Imagination. This is a building with a sense of its own importance, basking in the limelight.

The eerie central atrium has a soaring Gothic quality. Were the roof removed and the space left open to the elements, the resulting rain-drenched vista would be straight out of 'Blade Runner'.

Although Lloyd's looks as if it has been welded together from a thousand steel components, the frame was cast in concrete to meet fire safety requirements. (Water-filled steel tubes had been the architects' first choice.) Within the concrete structure, aluminium-framed modular panels hold sheets of dimpled glass, textured by passing through steel rollers, and everywhere the detailing is both highly engineered and beautifully finished. The modules, pods and pipes that festoon the outer surface are a result of the decision to banish all of the building's services to the exterior, leaving the interior open and flexible. Many of the components, such as the toilet capsules and staircase pods, were prefabricated elsewhere to a high degree of finish, and craned into place. This method speeded up construction, creating a muscular engine-room aesthetic and allows for services (lifts, lavatories, air-conditioning) to be upgraded with minimum disruption. Lloyd's is a building that can be overhauled, stripped down, upgraded and retuned.

If Le Corbusier intended to build 'machines for living', then Rogers has effectively created a machine for commerce, inward-looking and utterly focused. The central atrium is relatively narrow with the upper floors glazed to insulate against noise, creating a far less light-filled space than the ground floor would suggest. On a bright summer's day, the building is a glittering steel abstraction, its surfaces catching the movement of the sun reflecting the colour of the sky. But on a grey winter's morning, it resembles a hermetically sealed box, where workers are 'plugged in' at their desks to work, supplied with air to breathe and electricity for their machines. The communications stands loiter, like sentinels, their flickering screens trained upon the frantic traders. This is a scene not far removed far from Fritz Lang's vision of human drudgery in 'Metropolis' (1927), save for the promise of dry Martinis and champagne should the deals come off.

Rogers's building is brilliantly conceived and immaculately put together, combining the flexibility of prefabrication with the sense of permanence that a monument for an august financial institution requires. That it has not become the definitive blueprint for every office or apartment block in the western world suggests that both commissioning clients and architects are now looking to address peoples' needs for the sensuous and transparent, rather than simply driving for pure mechanical efficiency.

The web of escalators, their side panels glazed in a golden yellow, seem symbolic of the torrent of money that changes hands everyday, moving from floor to floor between the traders.

The lower floors overlook the main atrium, with its classical lantern holding the famous Lutine Bell. The communications stands loom like sentinels, endlessly patrolling the corridors on the lookout for workers failing to meet their productivity targets.

geometry has formed the basis for much of late twentieth-century architecture, the standardization of construction making the inclusion of regular geometric elements almost a foregone conclusion. However, precise geometry may not simply be a matter of the practical conveniences of repeating components, but representative of the architect's own artistic inclinations or belief in its spiritual significance. For Augustin Hernández, a prominent member of Mexico's architectural community, the use of geometry holds a deeper, almost mystic symbolism. For him, 'symmetry is orderly equilibrium'[3] and this is nowhere more apparent than with Casa Hernández.

The impetus for this exercise in geometrical gymnastics was a direct response to the problems of a site where houses already occupied the land on which it was easiest to build. Left with a steeply sloping plot, partially overshadowed by its neighbours, the only way the architect could fulfil his client's wish for 'a room with a view' was by creating a house in the air. The basic structure is formed by two upright walls, some 35 m (115 ft) high, running across the slope, which are pierced by four horizontal prisms that form the main part of the house, like immense white concrete Toblerones held captive within circular apertures in the uprights. The top and bottom edges of the four prisms are bolted to two massive beams, connected in turn to the inner faces of the apertures, allowing the prisms to seemingly hover within the rings. The lower beam extends back to connect the house to the hillside, providing the main point of access, while the top beam is staggered back to leave a balcony with dramatic views over Mexico City on the outer face, and a projecting canopy under which two cars can be parked at the rear. There is a basic symmetry to the building's profile that corresponds to the architect's theories about visual harmony being dependent on equilibrium. With the land

CASA HERNANDEZ

Above: A narrow footbridge dramatically crosses the void to enter a sliding door in one of the hollow uprights. Overhead, the bulk of the house seems to glide like a starship in the opening sequence of 'Star Wars Episode IV'.

Left: The side elevation clearly shows the house's composition, with the ground falling rapidly away below. The hard landscaping of the hillside has created sun terraces and a swimming pool, with the waterfall from this being just visible on the right.

Opposite: The startling geometry of the house gives the impression that it is moving, with the layered sections sliding back and forth, like a piece of futuristic kinetic sculpture.

ARCHITECT	Augustin Hernández
LOCATION	Bosques de las Lomas, Mexico City, Mexico
CREATED	1988–90

falling away sharply at 65 degrees, the house looks as though it is being projected into space despite having actually been tethered at its balance point.

Inside, the house is divided into five floors, with the main living rooms on the same level as the projecting balcony. The hollow concrete uprights contain wine cellars and stairs to the terraced gardens on the slopes, making maximum use of the structure. In contrast to the hard industrial look of the steel, glass and reinforced concrete exterior, the architect made extensive use of wood for the bespoke furniture and fittings. The floors are further separated at the front by a window that runs the full height of the house, dividing both the upper and lower sections to create the profile of the four prism ends. These Hernández describes as representing 'Four Seasons, Four Quadrants to the Day, Four Lunar Quadrants, Four Elements, Cosmic Rhythm, Dynamic Wheel of time, the Cycle of Returning Years.'[4]

Hernández's poetic essay in concrete symmetry bears a strong visual similarity to the more virtual worlds created by designers for the cult Disney film 'Tron' (1982), the first major, full-length feature film to employ computer-generated images (CGI). Imitating the basic wire-frame models and flat shaded planes of popular video games, the 'Tron' designers combined live-action

shot against black screens, with pioneering three-dimensional vector graphics – objects defined by coordinates that had to be entered by hand in order to make them move. As it took 600 coordinates to create just 4 seconds of film, the objects were simplified to true solids, moving around a wire-frame polygonal landscape. There is a remarkable visual correlation between Casa Hernández and the 'Recognizer Program', a flying machine with the extruded profile of triangles and oblongs. Hernández's own 1980s computer renderings of his design share the black backgrounds, coloured lines and faceted shading of the films' stills, while the way vehicles were animated to fragment upon crashing mirrors the house's staggered balconies and car ports.

This chance visual correlation highlights the role that increasingly sophisticated computer programs have played in forming both our real and virtual worlds, the appearance of both architecture and animation being dictated by the tools that create them. While films are being produced with ever-more fluid photorealistic CGI, adopting the advanced software of the aviation industries means that architects, too, are enjoying the freedom to create more expressive biomorphic forms. If Casa Hernández is the 'Tron' of architecture, then Frank Gehry's Guggenheim Bilbao is effectively the profession's 'Toy Story'.

The narrow void within one of the upright columns houses a staircase, whose white cantilevered treads spiral down like turbine blades to the terracotta cogs of the cellar's wine racks.

The immense glass windows between the two uprights allow for an uninterrupted view of the waterfall in the garden beneath.

At night the homeowner can sit like Lord Vader on the bridge of an immense Super Star Destroyer and look out over Mexico City through the full-height glazing that splits the building in two.

In the early 1990s, Zaha Hadid enjoyed an astonishing reputation as an architect, lecturer and painter. Having studied at the Architectural Association from 1972 and been awarded their Diploma Prize in 1977, she went on to hold various chairs and professorships at several US universities, including Harvard. Yet, paradoxically, despite having blazed a trail through the architectural consciousness for well over a decade, Hadid was not given the opportunity to realize any of her schemes, until an enlightened European furniture company made a decision to turn the accepted model of corporate architecture on its head.

It was a more literal blaze that destroyed a large part of the Vitra factory in 1981, beginning the sequence of events that led to Hadid's first commission. Vitra is a legend within the furniture industry and the manufacturer of some of the greatest twentieth-century design icons, including works by luminaries such as Charles and Ray Eames and Verner Panton. Nicholas Grimshaw was commissioned to design the sleek new replacement factory and to lay out a masterplan for the whole complex, but Vitra's purchase and installation in 1984 of a massive outdoor sculpture, 'Balancing Tools' (Claes Oldenburg & Coosje van Bruggen), made the company executive stop and reappraise their approach. Instead of a harmonious roll-out of refined but restrained

VITRA FIRE STATION

Left: At night the canopy over the garage door is silhouetted by careful back-lighting, drawing attention to its sharp fragmented form. The entrance to the station is just to the left of the main garage, where the building bends to follow the site.

Right: The rear elevation of the projecting arm containing the firemen's quarters displays the frameless flush mount glass used to preserve the purity of Hadid's graphic forms.

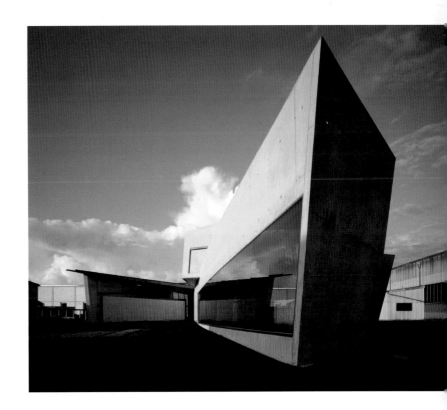

ARCHITECT	Zaha Hadid
LOCATION	Weil am Rhein, Germany
CREATED	1991–93

The prismatic angular aesthetic is continued inside by the polished steel-clad lockers that act as dividers screening the entrance to the toilets and changing rooms. A rich dash of colour is added by the gilded wall at the end of the corridor. Even the firemen's toilet cubicles are considered worthy of attention, having been given that distinctive lean common to most of Hadid's compositions.

Opposite: The sweeping expanse of the main garage, fully glazed from floor to ceiling, was designed to accommodate five fire-engines, but now comfortably displays Vitra's renowned collection of '100 Chairs', a highlight of the site's grand tour.

buildings, Vitra, under owner Rolf Fehlbaum, decided to commission different architects for each structure, beginning a new age of design patronage that had proved so successful in their furniture lines. Vitra steadily accumulated a clutch of cutting-edge buildings, bearing some of the most famous names in architecture, including such notable coups as Frank Gehry's first project in Europe, the Vitra Design Museum (1989). The result was not unlike a sculpture park (the concept that 'Balancing Tools' had introduced), acting as a draw to visitors, who toured the buildings to understand Vitra's history and design ethos, enhancing its image as an innovative style-maker.

Hadid's contribution to this architectural wonderland was originally to be three separate buildings (a bicycle shed, fire station and fire-exercise structure) but having explored the site, she decided to combine the elements in a single elongated building that defines the space by forming a natural boundary between the other structures, rather than simply floating (and possibly being lost) among the bulk of the factory halls. The building is almost entirely constructed from exposed reinforced concrete, carefully cast with sharp, crisp edges to enhance the deftly jutting planes and surfaces. These planes appear to slide past each other with the functions of the station occurring in the voids in-between. The kinetic quality of Hadid's architecture is tangible, like a frame of celluloid capturing a moment in time, creating an air of tension that evokes the concept of firemen poised at the alert waiting for the telephone to ring. The building bends in the middle, creating two separate wings; the firemen's quarters and the garage with its 32 m (105 ft) span giving an uninterrupted space in which to park the fire-engines. Its cantilevered external canopy dramatically stretches 12 m (39 ft) from the slender steel columns at its middle. Everywhere the detailing is kept to a minimum with sliding, rather than hinged, doors and frameless glass, all so as not to clutter the pure shards that Hadid has so carefully transposed into a three-dimensional form.

This accretion of graphic elements is part of Hadid's design process. Rather than drawing her buildings in plan, section and elevation, she prefers to create sketches and paintings that reflect how the viewer actually perceives a structure, instead of simply recording its dimensions to scale. By drawing freehand, she feels that she ascertains more about the building's character than can be deduced by conventional means, with chance discoveries generated through the drawing process feeding back into the design process.

Surprisingly, Hadid's first creation enjoyed only a short period of use as an operational fire station, Vitra perhaps feeling that it was all together too good a building to be left to perform such a utilitarian function. Since the late 1990s, the station's voluminous garage has housed Vitra's famous collection of '100 Chairs', the chairs presented in such a way as to elevate them to high art. This seems fitting, almost prophetic, given that Hadid has gone on to design more purpose-built treasure houses on a grander scale, such as the Rosenthal Contemporary Arts Center, Cincinnati (2003). The Vitra Fire Station proved to be both a successful corporate landmark and a useful starting point for an architect to transfer her art into the third dimension.

ARCHITECT	Santiago Calatrava
LOCATION	Lyons-Satolas Airport, Lyons, France
CREATED	1989–94

LYONS-SATOLAS TGV STATION

There can be little disagreement about Santiago Calatrava being an architect with the 'wow' factor. But then, he is not strictly an architect by training, but an outstanding civil engineer with an artistic flair, who has developed an international reputation for landmark buildings that can perhaps only be rivaled by that of Frank Gehry. Transportation has historically brought out Calatrava's best qualities; his competition-winning design for the Stadelhofen Railway Station in Zurich (1982) was followed in 1984 by the commission to design the Bach de Roda Bridge for the Barcelona Olympics, the first in a long line of bridge projects that have literally formed the backbone of his practice.

In 1989, the city of Lyons (France's second largest metropolitan area after Paris) launched a competition for the design of a new TGV terminal to link the rail and road networks to the Lyons-Satolas Airport with the aim of creating a 'grande' statement, a triumphal gateway for visitors landing on French soil. The TGV network is itself a modern marvel, with streamlined high-speed trains streaking through the French countryside at 300 km/h (186 mph) attracting envious attention from neighbouring countries.

The three converging arches are combined into a single concrete foot, or beak, that anchors the structure to the ground. The aesthetic is too hard-edged to be entirely organic, being an almost robotic interpretation of a living form.

Right: Passengers arriving at the station's west entrance have to pass under the predatory beak of the hawk as it dives down into the earth.

The delicate illuminated tracery of steel elements adds rhythm to the swooping bird at night, suggestive of metallic feathers swept back by passing trains and aircraft.

The ticket hall ceiling is a complex geometric form resting on concrete arches that were cast in situ, using twenty-five different sets of steel shuttering to achieve a smooth junction-free finish.

In his competition-winning entry, Calatrava proposed a building infused with the sense of excitement and glamour that once accompanied all air travel in the 1960s, before it ceased to be a novelty and devolved to become the mind-numbing assault course of check-in desks and luggage carousels. There is drama here on a par with Eero Saarinen's TWA terminal at JFK Airport (1956–62) and the two share forms that distill the essence of flight. Though the station can easily be interpreted as a swooping bird form, wings swept back and beak outstretched, Calatrava has always denied that this was his primary inspiration saying that his main reference point were his own studies in sculpture and the human form, particularly the eye. Making reference to our own anatomy is a common theme to his work, the City of Arts and Sciences being akin to a cluster of human features (see pp 60–65).

The ticket hall and concourse of the station dart out over the tracks, with two sunken platforms, 500 m (1,640 ft) long, extending to either side. The bulk of the station has been built below ground in anticipation that a runway extension would have to overlap the site, leaving the bird-like head of the ticket hall to dominate the landscape. This hall is formed by three sweeping steel arches, 120 m long and 40 m tall (394 x 131 ft) at their highest point, with the central arch having a triangular section that creates the backbone. This is connected to the outer tubular steel arches by diagonal bracing that forms a series of diamond-shaped glazed openings that admit natural light into the interior. The fanned sides of the ticket hall are also glazed between delicately splayed steel fingers, leaving the wings (or eyebrows) to seem to float above the concourse on a cushion of air. The structure's weight is borne by the three arches bearing down into concrete anchors, two being combined with lift shafts at the eastern end, while the third forms the organically moulded beak where the three arches converge. The platforms are reached by escalators from the raised concourse and are spanned by long lines of faceted concrete members that stretch out like racks of bleached prehistoric ribs. At their centre is a boxed concrete tunnel that allows express trains to whistle safely through the station at full speed without suction pulling passengers off their feet.

Lyons's TGV station is possibly the clearest example of how a building can become a work of sculptural beauty without sacrificing any of its legibility. Passengers are instinctively drawn through the spaces, all the while being treated to unfolding geometric vistas of glass, concrete and steel. Calatrava has produced a structure that has all the necessary qualities to be considered High-Tech sculpture, but without the inaccessible pretensions of contemporary modern art.

Top: The platform roof provides endless abstract geometric compositions that keep architectural photographers glued to their view-finders.

Above: A glance down the faceted colonnade of the platform shows how essential structural components can become refined sculpted forms that create complex abstract plays of light and shadow.

There can be few architectural styles that dovetail as neatly with a county's economy and culture as High-Tech does with Japan. The rise to postwar dominance of the island's electrical and automotive industries transformed it from war-torn former power to an international player. But whereas European High-Tech examples such as Lloyd's of London and the Centre Pompidou make clear reference to industrial processes and mechanical functions, the iconic Fuji-Sankei HQ Building seems to take the visual analogy down to the molecular level of atoms and particles.

The building was the penultimate work of Kenzo Tange, the greatest Japanese architect of the twentieth century and a leading light for over forty years. From strictly Modernist beginnings, Tange branched out into more expressive forms, but ended his career with highly geometric designs that appeared to be formal representations of atomic structures. The Fuji Building is a manifestation of ideas that Tange had been exploring since the 1960s as the figurehead of Japan's Metabolist group, who stressed the flexibility of a building over the final form, insisting that it should be able to evolve and adapt to meet changing needs.

The name 'Metabolist' derived from their interpretation of the biological process of building up or removing cells in living tissue, which they used as a metaphor for their flexible architecture. At much the same time as Archigram was publishing its famous montages in London (see pp 178–79), the Metabolists were developing their own obsession with pods, cells and other components that could be clipped onto basic frames to create 'megastructures'.

The Fuji Building is just such a megastructure, clearly visible from across Tokyo Bay, from its commanding position on the artificial island of Odaiba, overlooking the transport artery of the Rainbow Bridge. The islands were originally developed as defensive artillery forts in the 1850s (Odaiba literally meaning 'platform') in response to the threat posed by US Admiral Perry's 'Black Ships' that were attempting to force Japan to open itself up to trade. Considered obsolete by the 1920s, the forts and their surrounding area were turned into a National Park before further redevelopment in the 1980s as a purpose-built business district intended to satisfy Tokyo's insatiable demand for office space.

THE FUJI-SANKEI HQ BUILDING

Left: From the rear, the basic two-dimensional grid pattern becomes more readily apparent, rearing up like a mechanistic Mackintosh chairback.

Right: The illumination of the walkways at night transforms the structure into a giant pixilated gaming grid, upon which the sphere rests like an immense predatory Pacman.

ARCHITECT	Kenzo Tange Associates
LOCATION	Odaiba, Tokyo, Japan
CREATED	1993–96

The building's bulk is slightly deceptive, being composed of a grid with three tiers of elevated walkways connecting the two tower blocks. These aerial passages leave empty voids within the structure, suggesting that construction is still incomplete and that there is space available for further, inward expansion in correlation with Metabolist ideals. The space-frame is immensely strong, as the walkways act as box girders bracing the towers, helping the building resist Japan's frequent earthquakes. The structure itself comprises a steel frame with aluminium and glass cladding, a logical choice given the highly corrosive salt air of the bay in which it stands. The twenty-five-storey building rises four floors as one wedge-shaped block containing the main studios, before separating to become two distinct towers with the right being the office block and the left the media centre. The most striking feature is a gigantic sphere caught in the web of the walkways, like an immense projectile fired from the old artillery forts. Measuring 32 m (105 ft) in diameter, and clad in titanium in order to differentiate it from the rest of the structure, the sphere was preassembled on the ground and then jacked into position, its flashing aircraft-warning beacon topping out 123.5 m (405 ft) above the ground. The interior divides horizontally, the top hemisphere forming a domed public observation gallery and the lower half a restaurant with a machine room at its base. The company charges an admission fee to people wishing to experience the platform's unrivalled views of Tokyo Bay, but this does not deter the queues of waiting tourists that snake down the HQ's steps everyday.

Despite competition from what was (until the completion of the London Eye in 2000) the world's largest Ferris wheel, the Fuji Building is the islands' most distinctive landmark, its glittering sphere casting a watchful eye on the bay, looking at the container ships loaded with American goods that are now most welcome.

Fuji TV has fully exploited the potential of landmark architecture. The dark silhouette of the building at sunset gives the necessary futuristic element to the broadcaster's image, and has become part of their brand's iconography.

Right: The aluminium panels catch the sunlight, turning the building into a bewildering composition of lines and shadows more suggestive of an Escher rendering than a three-dimensional object.

In Sheffield, there lies evidence of a cautionary tale for politicians, architects and curators wishing to create provincial visitor attractions to emulate the popularity and success of Magna or The Deep. The former National Centre for Popular Music opened in March 1999, with the help of an £11 million National Lottery grant, but it had a short and troubled life that was perhaps only eclipsed by the dismal failure of the Millennium Dome.

At first, the concept seemed sound enough. Sheffield, like similar former industrial centres such as Liverpool and Manchester, had spawned numerous pop success stories such as Pulp, Def Leppard and Joe Cocker. In addition, it had been steadily developing a 'Cultural Industries Quarter' (CIQ), the largest in the region and home to around 450 organizations including Sony, Warp Records, Playstation and Time-Warner. With this wealth of both cultural activity and heritage, the stage seemed set for a music-oriented venue, full of interactive, hands-on exhibits.

But within seven months of opening, the gig had turned sour, with only a quarter of the anticipated 400,000 visitors making the trip to Sheffield. Despite desperate attempts to keep the centre open, it soon became insolvent and closed on November 2 1999, with debts of over £1 million pounds. The failure of the project was put down to its location and its contents, the vague notion of an interactive music 'experience' proving difficult to pin down and realize.

Thankfully, the story does not end there. By choosing to pick up on the city's heritage as a powerhouse of the steel, rather than musical, industry, Branson Coates produced a building that could successfully outlive its original purpose. The square plot was

NATIONAL CENTRE FOR POPULAR MUSIC

The four drums neatly occupy the square site with their lower floors glazed to meet the pavement. The upper floors were kept windowless to allow exhibition designers a completely controlled environment in which to create the 'experiences'.

ARCHITECT	Branson Coates
LOCATION	Sheffield, England
CREATED	1996–99

The powerful nozzles of the drums, with their precisely faceted forms, look ready to inhale the city, but are actually extracting the stale air from within.

Right: By separating the 'pods' with the vibrant orange web of the covered concourse, the architects presented the option of keeping the lower-floor cafés open to the public at night, after the exhibits had closed.

divided into four two-storey drums, each some 20 m (65 ft) across, linked by a glass-roofed cruciform concourse. The drums jostle each other, leaning at different angles on the sloping site like bulbous hovercraft loosely anchored to the ground. The illusion that they float is heightened by full-height glazing at street level, while their upper levels are clad in a pixilated fashion with 2,016 separate panels of ubiquitous Sheffield stainless steel, each 2 mm (1/10 in.) thick. The drums' nozzle-shaped roofs rotate in unison, like synchronized gun turrets on a vast Super Star Destroyer, tracking the prevailing breeze and contributing to the air-displacement ventilation system. The initial concept sketches mimicked mixing decks, with the vents being evolved from record player pick-up arms, but they are sufficiently refined so that the resulting building is not tied to those musical references.

Dividing the complex into eight separate but interconnected 'pods' over the two levels was originally intended to allow for constantly changing thematic exhibitions, but ultimately made it easier to finding a new use for the building when the 'pop experience' was over. After spending a short period as an alternative music venue, the building was sold for £1.85 million to Sheffield Hallam University in 2005, rechristened 'The Drum', and is now used as their Student Union. The 'hubs', as they are now referred to, act as offices, bars and music venues. Able to accommodate up to 220 people each, they are often hired out for corporate functions, a useful revenue stream that keeps the union self-sufficient.

The fact that the building made such a seamless transition after the centre's closure resonates with the architects' intention of creating 'soft architectures' that can adapt to the changing narratives they contain. They, at least, have emerged from the fiasco with credibility intact, leaving Sheffield with a distinctive landmark to be experienced by generations of students to come.

The Lowry was born out of local government's desire to effect a transformation of a former industrial area that would turn 'rivet guns to restaurants'. Paradoxically, the £105 million building charged with bringing about this change to Salford's grim townscape, bears the name of the artist who dedicated his life to recording all its grimy glory. L. S. Lowry, possibly the city's most famous son, came to live in Pendlebury near Salford when he was 22, and turned daily scenes of Northern grind into evocative paintings of smoking mills and factories populated by stick men and women. The Lowry sits on a triangular site at the end of Pier 8 in the docks – the terminus of the Manchester Ship canal – that could easily have been the scene of one of those paintings. Though once the vital artery of trade supplying goods directly into the city, the advent of containerization and ever larger ships meant that the canal soon became inadequate. Trade moved away from Salford Quays, resulting in rapid decline and eventual closure in 1982, leaving thousands unemployed.

Originally planned as the 'Salford Opera House', the project was re-designated an 'arts centre', in keeping with the spirit of anti-elitism that pervades many new music venues. Comparisons between Wilford's seemingly eclectic composition and that other metal-clad cultural beacon, the Guggenheim Bilbao, were inevitable, but the design ethos is quite different. Whereas Gehry's rip-roaring fanfare of titanium over steel is very much a product of his model-driven, sculptural approach, the Lowry is a highly rationalized composition. Given the complex and numerous roles that the building was to perform, Wilford conceived of a series of distinct forms, each housing a separate function, congregating within the triangular footprint of the site. Each would retain their own identity, and allow visitors to clearly discern the different sections, so avoiding the usual confusion of identical floor plans that can cause disorientation in large venues.

Visitors enter the building under an enormous dished canopy, its ends clad in perforated steel panels that make it appear solid by day only for it to transform at night with its girder structure illuminated from within. Inside the foyer a leaning wall of purple panels is punctured by vivid orange staircases that take audiences to the various tiers of seating. The sloping, steel-clad wedge that forms the main bulk of the structure is occupied by the Lyric Theatre, a versatile 1,730-seat auditorium with a striking blue, lavender and purple interior. This colouring provides a visual link with its exterior poking back into the foyer. A second smaller, 466-seat Quay Theatre cunningly backs onto its larger neighbour, allowing them to use the same backstage machinery.

THE LOWRY

Opposite: Wilford always intended this as a cultural beacon. The carefully conceived lighting makes the most of the reflective qualities of the neutral stainless-steel cladding and still waters of the dock.

Left: The character of the entrance changes dramatically at night when internal lighting transforms the canopy into a giant glowing radio telescope, exposing its internal structure.

ARCHITECT	Michael Wilford & Partners
LOCATION	Salford Quays, Manchester, England
CREATED	1997–2000

Left: A walk through the complex provides fantastical abstract views as the changing palette of textures and materials present themselves at every turn. Here the white concrete drum peeps through the spiralling curves of the tower.

Far left: The bold use of colour on the stairs above the foyer contrasts with the more restrained exterior. Wilford has created memorable forms and spaces that aid navigation through what could so easily have been a warren of uniform corridors.

Below: During the day the perforated steel ends of the entrance canopy carry no hint of the drama that unfolds when they are illuminated.

Right: The vivid colour and internal steel cladding add a sense of high drama to the Lyric Theatre even before the performers have come on stage.

The building's ultimate success is largely down to this architect-designed flexibility, which supports the ambitious and inventive events programme that has been staged since it opened, with over 250,000 more visitors than anticipated during its first year alone.

Elsewhere, various cylindrical and rhomboid forms house the other building's other functions, including the necessary rehearsal and dressing rooms with art spaces for changing exhibitions and of course, the Lowry Gallery. The funnel-like tower that forms the peak of the composition is far less substantial than the materials would suggest, with its light diamond lattice structure exposed by the spiralling steel cladding ending short of the top. The tower forms an exterior skin to a white concrete drum that houses The Lowry Collection (the largest in the world, numbering over 340 of his paintings and drawings), a selection of which is displayed in rotation in the galleries below.

The opportunity to develop the entirety of Salford Quays in line with Wilford's masterplan was sadly ditched, and instead of a public plaza ringed by cafés and restaurants, the Lowry's sweeping entrance gazes out onto a soulless multi-storey carpark. Despite this, Wilford has succeeded in integrating many diverse functions to produce a striking building that shows how good architecture can still thrive in less than ideal circumstances.

From its early genesis in Victorian Britain, the railway station has always been an important opportunity for a city or country to make a good first impression. From the then unprecedented wrought-iron spans of Brunel's terminus at London Paddington, to the sweeping glazed concourse of Nicholas Grimshaw's Eurostar Terminal at Waterloo, British architects have contributed a rich seam of architectural panache to the station genre, combining audacious engineering excellence with gracious forms. With the Singapore Expo Station, Foster & Partners have added to this long legacy, and provided Singapore not only with a triumphant gateway to a city, but a physical proclamation of an entire country's aspirations for the twenty-first century.

The new station is the first stop along the Changi Airport Line into Singapore itself, serving as a disembarkation point for the thousands of visitors that come to the events staged at the purpose-built, 25-hectare (62 acres) Expo complex. With such a large venue, the station's design had to be capable of accommodating an estimated 17,000 people per hour passing through its turn-styles at peak periods. The problems associated with such high densities of passengers are exacerbated by Singapore's climate, one of the warmest and, at 90 per cent humidity, dampest in the world. The country's heavy rainfall, high midday temperatures and the site's proximity to the sea with its associated corrosive marine salts, all presented challenges for both structure and materials.

The station is dominated by two floating forms rising above the raised railway tracks that sit in cast concrete viaducts, keeping the electrified lines free from potential inundation by torrential rains. An elongated blade form, 200 m (656 ft) long and derived from the section of a torus, rests over a central platform that is perched on concrete arches bridging the gap between the two railway lines. The blade itself only touches the ground via two pairs of V-shaped

EXPO STATION

Left: Caught in motion, like a flying saucer straining at its moorings, the disc hovers over the elevated railway lines, drawing attention to the station amidst the large monolithic exhibition halls.

Right: The iconic image of the station at night, an alien beacon guiding trains along the twin railway lines converging on the platform beyond.

ARCHITECT	Foster & Partners
LOCATION	Singapore
CREATED	1997–2001

concrete columns, elegant structural devices that create a minimum footprint at ground level, leaving space for the hordes of passengers to circulate. The relatively minor supporting role of the V-shaped columns is made possible by the canopy's own inherent rigidity, which is down to its diagrid structure of prefabricated steel sections interlocking to form a web of diamonds and triangles. This is so stable that it spans a 70 m (230 ft) gap at its widest point over the platforms, with its tips cantilevered 37 m (121 ft) at each end, and bears an uncanny resemblance to the Rebel Freighters from 'The Empire Strikes Back' (1980).

The blade's roof is clad with titanium sheet, chosen for its durability and capacity to reflect the baking sun. The platforms were deliberately left unenclosed, while the ground-floor ticket hall has latticed stainless-steel screens instead of walls, encouraging natural convection currents to draw fresh air up through the building. This combination creates a micro-climate within the station that can be as much as 4°C lower than that outside. The underside of the blade is a magical animated surface that catches every movement of the passengers beneath and ripples with colour as the red, striped trains pull in. Triangular panels are formed into diamond clusters that correspond to the diagrid structure, with those made from polished stainless steel acting as lights scoops reflecting daylight into the interior.

The most theatrical element is undoubtedly the 40 m (131 ft) wide disc, a hovering saucer on four stilt-like legs clad in satin-finished stainless steel. It is the disc that announces the station's presence across the flat Expo plain, in the same way as Charles Holden's brick towers advertised the presence of his 1930s London Underground stations. The tube running through its centre is topped with a skylight of diffuse glass and is directly aligned above the glass-and-steel lift from the ticket hall to the platform concourse. The effect is that of a teleporter, transferring passengers at warp speed to the waiting trains.

With their Jubilee station at Canary Wharf (1998), Foster & Partners had already proved that they had mastered the art of the station buried deep in the earth. With the Expo project, they have proved to be equally at home in the air.

The overlap between the disc and the blade provides an ongoing light show, with the rippling wave patterns around the disc's aperture giving the illusion of a time warp before passengers are beamed off the planet.

Bottom: From the ticket hall, the view of the top of the glass-walled lift shaft with the disc's tube directly above is one of pure science fiction.

The long slot cut through the centre of the platform provides a visual link between the ticket hall and trains while aiding the free circulation of air through the station. Passengers emerging from the escalators are treated to the glittering diamond patterns of the blade's polished underbelly.

ARCHITECT	Wilkinson Eyre Architects
LOCATION	Rotherham, South Yorkshire, England
CREATED	1998–2001

MAGNA SCIENCE ADVENTURE CENTRE

There is an inherent drama to the making of steel; the intense heat, the sparks, the searing white glow of molten metal flowing from the vast crucibles on its way to become anything from cars to cans. But when an industry leaves, as it did in Rotherham in 1993, after seventy-six years of production, what remains behind grows dark and still. But the two looming main sheds of the former Templeborough Steelworks, each enclosing a bay some 350 m long by 25 m high and wide (1148 by 82 ft), have been brought back to life by the skillful intervention of architects Wilkinson Eyre who have transformed the vast space into a informative adventure for young and old alike.

Nestling amongst the vast rusting hulks of the original machinery are exquisite shiny gems, carefully conceived pavilions devoted to each of Aristotle's four elements of the world: earth, air, fire and water. Linked together by walkways suspended from the existing structure, these pavilions form beacons in the dark. The very theatricality of the space has been enhanced by careful lighting devised by Speirs & Major, to create an atmosphere more akin to the director James Cameron's 1986 film 'Aliens' than to an family-orientated educational facility. Visitors stare out of the glowing pavilions, like Ripley scanning a dark, forbidding hulk for her acid-blooded adversaries. The brutal forms of machine components exposed to a harsh environment lie cold and quiet in the dark environment where it does not pay to look too deeply into the shadows. The urge to hire this as a venue for a futuristic paintball game is almost irresistible.

With their considered layout, the architects have captured some of the essence of the flowing, non-stop nature of the concaster process that used to be performed here. In this method, a reservoir of molten steel, fresh from the arc furnace, was water-cooled until it formed a hard skin, before being passed through the machine's various rollers while still molten at its core, to end up as blooms or slabs as required. What were once two distinct processes of casting and forging were combined into one continuous action. Similarly, young explorers pick their way through dark cavernous space, venturing cautiously from base to base to learn about each

element through a series of interactive displays, with the story of steel and its production threaded in between.

The most dramatic of the four pavilions are Air and Water. The former appears to hover like a latter-day Zeppelin, pierced by a steel walkway some 40 m (131 ft) long, and suspended 12.5 m (41 ft) above the ground. Engineered by Vector Special Projects, it shares its inflated skin of ETFE (ethylene tetrafluoroethylene) with the biomes of the Eden Project to which the company also contributed. The material is used here not to admit light to plants, but as a metaphor for air that allows the exhibition designers to project footage of changing weather patterns onto its inner surface.

The Water Pavilion takes the form of a twisted roll of corrugated stainless steel, rolled like a wave of fluid cascading through an Archimedes screw and lit at both ends by cold cathode tubes mounted on swooping steel ribs. Waist-high tanks of water, used to feed the moving exhibits, act as a bulkhead at the pavilion's entrance giving visitors the sense that they are being immersed in their subject.

This is the architecture that carried off the coveted £20,000 Stirling Prize in 2001, after seeing off competition from none other than the Eden Project (see pp 166–69). 'Steel trumps Trees' as it were. Wilkinson Eyre went on to win the Stirling Prize again the following year with the Gateshead Millennium Bridge, a controversial decision in the eyes of some who feel that bridges are not architecture, and are best credited to the engineers who make them possible. However, the triumphant success of the Magna is not so contested, and it has become a much-needed tourist attraction for a region that remains in industrial decline.

Far left: The Air Pavilion, seemingly suspended in mid-air by its web of cables that hold the ribs of membrane taut, is actually supported by four box beams connected to the steel walkway.

Below left: The original gantries and hoists are poised over the carefully detailed carpark, as if prepared to playfully shuffle the vehicles while their owners are inside.

Right: The Water Pavilion appears small and sleek compared to the rusting right angles of its surroundings. At its peak of production in the 1950s, this vast space provided a workplace for 10,000 men, but since opening has attracted an average of 300,000 visitors a year.

Overleaf: At the entrance visitors pass through the eerily illuminated concrete tunnel into the nine-storey-high space where they find themselves facing one of the largest light walls in Europe, 35 by 8 m (115 by 26 ft) high-rise of polycarbonate panels emitting a warm pink glow.

The Bibliotheca Alexandrina is an attempt to recreate the legacy of the original Library of Alexandria, begun in 288 BC by Ptolemy I, a Macedonian general who seized Egypt in the power vacuum created by the death of Alexander the Great. The strong Hellenistic tradition continued with such luminaries as Archimedes acting as custodians for its estimated 700,000 manuscripts and papyri before they were finally destroyed towards the end of the fourth century AD. The ambitious idea to resurrect one of Egypt's lost wonders was proposed back in 1974 by Professor Mahdouh Lofti Diware, President of the University of Alexandria, who convinced the Egyptian Government that such a project would be a regional centre of excellence, which could lead to an education-led economic revival of the Middle East. The project was launched with an international competition in 1989, which received an unprecedented 524 entries. The winning design was the work of the relatively unknown Norwegian practice Snøhetta (literally 'Snow-hut'), and when the library was finally opened in 2000, it had cost an estimated US $220 million. It is capable of storing half a million open-access books, with a further eight million in the closed stacks.

The library takes the basic form of a cylinder, sliced through obliquely at sixteen degrees, and tilted so that the lowest edge sinks 12 m (39 ft) beneath the ground while the other rises 32 m (105 ft) into the air. The sixteen-degree sloping face appears as a giant disc, rising above the horizon as though it is tilted to the sun, following its every movement. In reality, its purpose is to ensure that the interior receives no direct light that would fade spines and raise temperatures. The roof's grid is comprised of rectangular bays, subdivided into triangular sections made from aluminium, with one bent down to form a level surface and the other matching the slope of the roof. Northern light is reflected off the sunken lower triangles through anti-UV glazed windows to bounce off the ceiling under the upper triangle, and, so diffused, is allowed down into the interior. The light is needed to illuminate the great reading room, a cavernous space some 160 m (525 ft) in diameter with fourteen terraced platforms capable of accommodating 2,200 users at any time. The roof is supported by 20-tonne concrete beams resting on a multitude of slender columns with flared precast capitals, seemingly making reference to the veritable jungles of lotus-topped columns found in the temples of Karnak and Luxor.

The references to Egypt's past are more readily apparent on the exterior of the south-facing wall, a cooling thermal mass that acts like a shield to protect the library from the intense Egyptian sun. This imposing façade is composed of 4,600 light grey, riven Aswan granite blocks, upon which letters from the alphabets of the world – from cuneiform to Braille – have been incised. The architects strove for a form that would give the library a timeless quality, as befitting a building intended as a lasting monument to Middle Eastern culture and learning. The sphere and disc are both symbols rooted in Egyptian mythology as representations of the sun god Ra, pre-eminent among the immortals, and, though the architects denied that this was their inspiration, it was a

BIBLIOTHECA ALEXANDRINA

Left: At night, the illuminated swirls of the part-submerged Planetarium give the illusion that it is rolling towards the sea. It acts as a beacon marking the end of the entrance ramp to the library beyond.

Right: The foot of the tilting north-facing façade rests against a retaining wall, which counter-balances the massive weight of the south-facing granite shield and holds back the water of the harbour just across the road.

ARCHITECT	Snøhetta
LOCATION	Alexandria, Egypt
CREATED	1998–2002

convenient metaphor with which to describe the structure to Middle Eastern benefactors.

Perhaps the most futuristic element of the complex is the 18 m (59 ft) diameter concrete sphere of the Planetarium on the approach to the library. It hangs, dramatically suspended on its axis, over a pit in the form of a glazed inverted pyramid that houses an adjoining Science Museum. The design is said to have been inspired by the first photograph of the Earth taken from the moon.

With its juxtaposition of ancient carvings and high-tech, machined forms, the library successfully fuses ancient with modern, evoking both Egypt's past glories and contemporary ambitions. Its aesthetics seem reminiscent of those devised for the film 'Stargate' (1994) and its spin-off television series, but without a hint of artificiality. Whereas the film's frenzy of hieroglyphic-strewn scenery, flying pyramids and 'Pharaohs in Space' is pure fiction, the Bibliotheca Alexandrina's archives offer a more realistic form of time travel via the written word. If this centre for learning develops as Professor Diowar hopes, then the library could well reassert the Middle East's claim to be the cradle of civilization.

Above left and right: The groves of columns support the concrete beams into which blue and green glass lanterns have been set. Patterns of coloured light are projected onto the reading desks, moving with the sun as it tracks across the roof.

Right: The sweeping curve of the south façade bearing the characters from all the world's languages is the element that provides the structure's most literal connection to the spirit of its past incarnations.

When viewed directly from its base, the sloping disc of the reading room roof is a mass of the converging perspective lines, clearly showing the grid pattern of the triangular sun traps.

THE DEEP

The decision to build The Deep, one of a clutch of high-profile Millennium projects, was always very much a local affair. The brainchild of the city's Director of Leisure, Colin Brown and the Chair of the Tourism Committee, Councillor David Gemmell, it was envisaged from the outset as an icon for Hull. Their choice of a learning centre focused on the sea tallied perfectly with the town's strong maritime and fishing heritage, both now in sharp decline. But this was not to be simply an aquarium, a mere collection of tanks containing fish, but something far more ambitious. The world's first 'submarium', with the oceans in microcosm acting like a magnet for tourists and scientists alike, a catalyst for the town's regeneration. Brown's working title of 'The Deep' soon stuck, echoing the ambition of the scheme.

With his competition-winning design, Sir Terry Farrell has surely fulfilled that brief, creating a building that so resonates with cultural and historical nuances that it cannot fail to be associated with Hull. The shape is squat and purposeful, quite appropriate on a site where its design capability for withstanding 100mph winds and tidal surges may well be tested. The hard edges and angular form hark back to the triangular citadel that once occupied the same ground. The extensive use of marine-grade aluminium cladding, and the sharp, prow-like nose resemble the tankers that navigate along the Humber. The building sits purposefully like a seal on a rock, but with a vague hint of predatory shark.

All these associations are welcomed, but the real driving inspiration behind the form was geological. Early on in the design process, Farrell formed the idea of the building rising, like a shard through the Earth's crust, thrusting its way to the surface. This 'tectonic' look was maintained throughout the development, though it evolved considerably. The cladding was changed from

The Deep gives a predatory glance at passing shipping, as if contemplating whether to dive in and attack. The parallels between a long tanker and the prow-nosed building are clear to see.

ARCHITECT	Terry Farrell & Partners
LOCATION	Kingston upon Hull, England
CREATED	1998–2002

The deliberately layered effect of the cladding makes direct reference to Farrell's initial concept; the building should embody the history of the oceans, which is found in the fossilized remains on Earth.

The seemingly random, faceted cladding is reminiscent of the dazzle camouflage employed to disguise convoy ships in World War II to avoid the attentions of preying U-boats.

Below: The floor-to-ceiling windows of the main tank really bring the depths into view. The massively thick acrylic sheets were ordered when work began on site and the roof had to be left off to allow them to be craned into position.

Bottom: From the glazed nose section, 24 m above sea level, and partially open to the elements, visitors are treated to dramatic views of the confluence of the rivers Hull and Humber.

giant 8 x 4 m (26 x 13 ft) stainless-steel panels, to 4 x 2 m (13 x 6.5 ft) machine-cut, marine-grade aluminium. The smaller panels – the largest dimensions available in that material – made for easier construction and greater precision with tolerances of just 1.5 mm ($\frac{1}{32}$ in.). The carefully chosen layers of colour and pattern, punctuated with fissure-like windows, clearly convey the concept of exposing geological strata. This futuristic building, with its carefully sequenced exhibitions, is a time-travelling machine, taking visitors through the history of our oceans in a slice of the Earth's crust.

If the building looks heavy and muscular, it is by necessity. The concrete substructure, with its piles extending 30 m (98 ft) into the peninsula, cradles the deepest single aquarium tank in Europe, at some 10 m (33 ft). Around this, the building has a substantial frame, composed of between 1,700 and 1,800 separate members, almost 800 tonnes (882 tons) of structural steel in all. The volumes involved are gigantic. At any one time, the building contains 2,850,000 litres (627,000 gallons) of water. The 'skimmer' tower, part of the water-purifying process, is the largest in the world, with the capacity to ensure that the 2,800 marine creatures are kept in ideal conditions. The exhibition route takes visitors from the naturally lit top-floor lobby down into the dark mysterious depths, made to look even deeper by careful lighting. The walkways and exhibits inhabit the voids created by the tanks, which Farrell relates to the natural fissures caused in rocks by water erosion or time. The climax of the tour is the dramatic glass lift that whisks visitors up from the depths, and through the main tank they have been glimpsing along the way.

The Deep's unqualified success can be measured in its visitor numbers alone. The cautious Brown and Gemmell had insisted that the financial break-even should be set at a predicted 200,000 visitors annually. By the end of the first quarter alone, over 250,000 had been inducted into the depths, and The Deep continues to make waves.

THE FALKIRK WHEEL

The 8 m (26 ft) diameter cog of the central axle protrudes from the pier that holds the machinery. Each gondola is mounted in an identical cog, with two smaller cogs linking the three in a line to create the turning motion that keeps them level.

ARCHITECTS	RMJM Architects Ove Arup Butterley Engineering
LOCATION	Falkirk, Scotland
CREATED	1999–2002

At first glance, a proposal for a boatlift to connect two separate Scottish canals would seem like an improbable structure for inclusion in a book on futuristic architecture. After all, canals were the cutting-edge technology of the eighteenth-century, rather than the twenty-first. But in the hands of a consortium of companies including the world-famous Ove Arup Consultants and the Edinburgh-based architects RMJM, this £84.5 million project is arguably one of the most dynamic and successful schemes to emerge from the Millennium Commission's funding initiative.

The problem facing the engineers was to find an efficient method of transferring pleasure craft 35 m (115 ft) down from the Union Canal to the Forth & Clyde Canal and back up again. Normally this is achieved by 'staircases', or flights of locks, but these are slow and consume vast amounts of precious water. The design team reworked the original concept of a Ferris wheel with several gondolas to create one of the most staggeringly beautiful engineering feats in the canal world. From a central axle spread two pairs of arms, their distinctive futuristic spurs suggesting movement even when stationary. In their ringed 'hands' are held two identical gondolas, each capable of taking two boats up to 20 m (66 ft) long. Boats on the Union Canal emerge from a tunnel in the side of the hill and approach the gondolas along a reinforced concrete aqueduct supported on piers with ringed tops that echo the arms of the lift. Once the watertight doors have been sealed, ten hydraulic motors rotate the arms with the gondolas, which are kept horizontal by a simple system of cogs geared around the central axle. The Archimedes Principle – a vessel will displace its own weight in water – determines that both gondolas weigh the same, even when only one boat is being transported. The arms are so well balanced that the amount of electrical energy required to make one turn is only 1.5 kWh, the equivalent of boiling just eight kettles of water.

For such a piece of high-tech engineering, the wheel has a satisfyingly rugged appearance, enhanced by the use of specially made bolts (over 15,000 of them) to link the 1,200 tonnes of steel components together. This construction method has much in common with the style of engineering used by the original Victorian canal engineers and is reminiscent of Brunel's massive bridges, or Stephenson's locomotives. It is how Jules Verne's dreams of space travel were visualized by the illustrators of the day, studded with rivets, cog teeth bared, oozing muscular confidence. The decision to use bolts was not, however, a flight of fancy, but the most robust solution to the immense and constantly shifting stresses that the gondolas are subjected to. Normal welded joints that give modern metal structures their sleek streamlined appearance would simply have been far too susceptible to fatigue.

The wheel is not only a means of conveying boats, but also a draw to tourists, who can sit insulated from the often inclement Scottish weather in the visitors' centre built in the lift's shadow.

Taking the form of an orange segment, the centre's sloping
glazed roof affords quite unsettling views as the lift rotates,
its gondolas seemingly about to fall through the glazing before
grazing by. Those with a head for heights can also take a ride on
the wheel itself on one of the frequent boat tours, enjoying the
spectacular views the lift affords during the 4 minutes it takes
to complete the ascent.

In the Falkirk Wheel, Scotland now boasts the world's first
rotating boatlift, a structure that is both functional and sculptural,
and which takes the art of transportation engineering quite
literally up a level.

The geometrical simplicity of the
structure adds to the clarity of its
operation, the ringed 'hands' cradling
the boats gently down to the basin
below. The still waters produce
reflections that appear to double
the lift's height.

ARCHITECT	Rem Koolhaas/OMA
LOCATION	Porto, Portugal
CREATED	1999–2005

CASA DA MUSICA

For a city looking to revive its fortunes, there seems to have been a decades-long trend for commissioning pieces of landmark architecture to act as beacons for regeneration. Porto, Portugal's second city and home of the internationally famous wine to which it gives its name, was a city with just such aspirations when it launched a belated competition to design a home for the National Orchestra of Porto as part of the town's tenure as European City of Culture in 2001. The restrictive time-scale attracted only three competition entries, from which the design by Rem Koolhaas and his Office for Metropolitan Architecture (OMA) was selected. Three changes of city government and five different Casa da Musica Directors made for further delays, but the opera house finally opened in April 2005.

The final building is the complete antithesis of the accepted opera house form. Instead of an august pillar of the establishment, Koolhaas has delivered a faceted monolith in precision-moulded white concrete that leans precariously like some cantilevered geometric boulder over a square paved in rusty Jordanian travertine. The unusual form was originally designed at a more modest scale. Koolhaas liked his earlier unrealized design for a private house in Rotterdam – which divided male and female spaces around a communal room – so much that he scaled it up five times to become an opera house. Here the auditorium similarly provides the meeting place for audience and musicians, while keeping them segregated elsewhere. This is the opposite approach to that of Foster's Sage in Gateshead, where the envelope of the building and layout of the auditoriums encourages performers to mix freely with their audiences (see pp 170–73).

The building towers 40 m (131 ft) above the plaza, the face adjacent to the entrance leaning out at an impressive sixty degrees. Remarkably, it is held in position not by extensive underground shoring, but by counter-balancing the weights of its various cast concrete faces. The roof is included in this complex equation (engineered by Cecil Balmond and his team at Arup), so the props that supported the sides during construction could not

Above and left: The flush-glazed window that backs onto the stage of the main auditorium is raised up by the sharply angular form, lifting it well above the surrounding streets. In contrast, windows at ground level allow passers-by to spy on musicians in the rehearsal rooms.

Right: Dwarfed by the scale of the building, visitors must climb up the concrete stair and enter through the aperture cut into its side, scurrying in like nervous Jawas boarding their ungainly angular sandcrawlers in the 'Star Wars' epics.

The plywood walls, with their oversized, gold-leaf grain, are outshone by a fake Baroque organ case made largely from fibreglass; a cost-cutting concession needed to keep within the project's £51 million budget.

be removed until the roof had been cast in situ. The walls then extend a further 15 m (49 ft) below the surface to contain the three underground floors holding the soloists' rehearsal rooms, insulating them from the noise of the carpark below the plaza.

This balanced form contains two auditoriums, the larger being 1,300 seats in the well-tried 'shoe box' arrangement that is widely agreed by musicians worldwide to give the best acoustics. Unusually for a music venue, Koolhaas chose to glaze both ends of the main auditorium, opening it up to the world outside. This challenges the conventional wisdom that such performance spaces should be sealed boxes, free from the distractions of the great outdoors. At night the building appears like a giant projector beaming culture out into the city through its apertures. The interior finishes continue the exterior's unconventional theme with a dizzying palette of materials that seems more akin to a Philippe Starck-designed hotel than an opera house. The main auditorium is clad in rough plywood, over which is applied gold leaf in the magnified pattern of its grain, catching the light coming through the full-height glazing at each end. A double wall with sections of specially designed waveform glass seals off each end, its undulating surface helping the acoustics within and dampening noise from outside. Around the auditoriums, the corridors and practice rooms are arranged like channels hollowed out of a giant irregular iceberg by running water. The effect for first-time patrons trying to find the way to their seats can be disorientating, but their visit could never be described as dull.

Porto's new opera house seems to have bottled the excitement of Koolhaas' architecture in the hope that it will prove to be a profitable vintage for years to come.

Above: The internal circulation spaces are a chaotic labyrinth of metal staircases that zigzag up through the building, following the geometry of the envelope.

Right: Above the main auditorium hovers a suspended frame with a PVC canopy, designed to inflate and deflate to adjust the acoustical resonance of the space according the style of music that is being performed.

PHAENO SCIENCE CENTRE

Top: Suggestive of the meteor-pocked hulk of a spaceship steadily cruising through the far reaches of the galaxy, the carefully cast slanting lines of the exterior panels give the heavy elongated building exterior a sense of gentle motion at night.

Right: The 'teleporter' – the lights of the coffee bar glare out of the cavernous undercroft. At night, the space is lit by fluorescent tubes hidden in the ceiling coffers, which also serves to lighten the floor slab as it rests on the cones.

ARCHITECT	Zaha Hadid
LOCATION	Wolfsburg, Germany
CREATED	2001–05

Wolfsburg was built in 1938 for the express purpose of housing the workers required to manufacture the Volkswagen, the 'people's car' that Hitler hoped would throng the autobahns of Germany. In the same way that the Volkswagen has managed to shrug off its past and be reincarnated as the friendly Beetle, Wolfsburg has begun a quest for a new identity in recognition that its manufacturing industry (so far its raison d'être) may one day decline in face of stiff competition from the East. The local council began a marketing campaign to rebrand the town as a strategic centre for science, technology and research, staging an international competition to design a science museum that could infuse the next generation with a desire for scientific exploration. Phaeno, a Greek word meaning to 'discover' or 'cast light upon', was eventually chosen as the project title, expressing the need for the project to convey an engaging sense of wonder. In Zaha Hadid's winning design, Wolfsburg found that wonder, a futuristic

vision that shrugs off the preconceptions of what a museum should be.

Hadid's success in the Wolfsburg competition was one in a string of seven victories between 1999 and 2001 that transformed her office from a studio of 15 into a major architectural firm employing 120 people. Her largest realized project at that time, Phaeno marked the maturing of a style that had evolved over decades of teaching and lecturing, turning the confident sweep of her atmospheric paintings into a leaping monolith of considerable weight. As in her Vitra Fire Station scheme, Hadid addressed the topography of the site, and the loosely triangular plan is determined by the intersection of road and rail links. The design, floating 7 m (23 ft) above street level on ten inverted concrete cones, is set amid a landscaped park of dunes and craters. By elevating the building on its irregular feet, like concrete vortexes sucked down from the floor slab above, Hadid deliberately created

By choosing to open up the floor, Hadid
exposes the double layer of the cones,
with a staircase threading its way in
between.

additional space beneath, an unexpected bonus that attracted the judges' attention. Hadid's vision was for this to become a public room, an artificial landscape under fluorescent stars that would make the centre a social focal point for the local population. The building's undulating undercroft was made possible by the extensive use of self-compacting concrete (SCC), the largest application of this material in Europe at the time. Whereas conventional concrete requires extensive vibration in order for it to settle and expel any air pockets, SCC has an ad-mixture of superplasticizer and stabiliser that improves the material's flow qualities and allows it to be poured directly into complex formwork.

The use of both SCC and pre-cast vibrated concrete can clearly be seen in Phaeno's façades; the sharp, crisp edges of the slab-sided walls contrast with the curvaceous underbelly of the floor slab upon which they rest. Hadid plays a visual game, pushing the materials to their limits in order to achieve the desired forms. The cones are not solid structures, but inhabited by access points, cafes and shops, as well as the more mundane building services. Six cones support the weight of the floor while the remaining four extend upwards to support the roof. This is a non-symmetrical grid, made from 4,700 different steel elements cut by CNC machinery and laid over the main space, leaving it uncluttered and open plan. The architects deliberately increased the visual weight of the ceiling, beyond pure structural necessity, using its converging perspective lines to emphasize the vast interiors.

Inside, the exhibits are scattered like oversized children's toys over an immense carpet where young visitors can explore in all

directions at will, rather than by a prescribed route. The hands-on nature of the exhibits is perfectly in keeping with Wolfsburg's history of practical engineering. The undulating floor, seamlessly cast in poured resin, makes for a surreal moonscape even more unworldly than the concrete plaza outside, with areas being defined not by static walls but by flowing ramps, dunes and craters, at some points made more intimate by changes in ceiling height formed by the undulations in the steel grid.

In Phaeno, Hadid has been given the opportunity to realize her theories on a grand scale and create a landmark building that is a magical hybrid of sculpture and architecture. The seamless merging of mass, space and structure makes for a building every bit as fluid as her competition-winning paintings promised.

Top: The rolling swells of the main floor are occasionally interrupted by handrails, like delicate steel breakwaters on a pure white beach. The ridges form and contain different spaces without having to resort to conventional partitions.

Above: The undulating chasm opens up for the exhibit where visitors get to play Zeus and make their own lightning.

RETURN OF
THE BLOB

MAC (Museu de Arte Contemporânea), Brazil

Millennium Dome, England

NatWest Media Centre, England

Spaarne Hospital Bus Station, the Netherlands

The Eden Project, England

The Sage, England

Selfridges, England

Kunsthaus Graz, Austria

Swiss RE, England

'Any sufficiently advanced technology is indistinguishable from magic.'

Arthur C. Clarke, 'Profiles of the Future', 1961 (Clarke's Third Law)

The Sleek, the Sensuous and the Sustainable

Few feats of human endeavour have ever matched the drama of the 1969 moon landings. For a whole generation, the grainy black and-white pictures on their television sets, beamed back to Earth from the cratered surface, appeared to announce a new dawn for mankind. It opened up the seemingly limitless possibilities that this infinite horizon might hold, fuelling a spirit of optimism that permeated all areas of art, architecture and design. Televisions in the shape of astronaut's helmets, Lava lamps cum Saturn Rocket and Bubble Houses like lunar-landing pods; a continuous flow of brightly coloured plastic and shiny chrome poured out of the factories of the world to feed the public's insatiable demand for all things cosmic.

For the members of the British architectural group Archigram, it must have seemed like a glorious vindication of their belief in modern technology to bring about a new era in building design. Their struggle to overcome the staid world of post-war Britain had begun as little more than a handful of sketches and poems printed on single sheets of the cheapest paper. They sold just 300 of them in 1961 at 9 pence each, but by 1969 they were selling thousands of thick, stapled issues all over the world. The group had so grown in size and stature as to be considered one of the most dynamic think-tanks of the age. That sense of movement and exploration that the Space Race embodied, came out in their proposals, such as Ron Herron's nomadic 'Walking Cities'; giant reptilian blobs on telescopic legs, striding across the landscape. In a world where ockets could travel at over 15,000 mph, not even a city was allowed to stand still, and in Archigram's bright Pop-Art layouts the future seemed so tantalizingly close.

But for all their inventive sketches and articulate essays, Archigram became most famous for building very little. They dared to dream, but no clients dared to commission them. When the practice broke up in 1974, it seemed that the Establishment may have won after all. The world simply wasn't ready for their ideas.

Fast forward to the late 1990s and the world had become a different place. There were no qualms then about using technology, for it is technology that is at the heart of this chapter. It is only with recent advances in computer science that many of these structures became possible, and once architects and engineers had harnessed the powerful software to do their bidding, then architecture began to make the quantum leap into the unknown. The architects who grew up in the golden age of space exploration can now fulfill their boyhood ambitions and build their dreams. For former Archigram colleagues, Peter Cook and Colin Fournier, this technology has come as a last-minute reprieve, the chance to make good on the promises sketched out all those years ago. The Kunsthaus is not just part of a renaissance for Graz; it is a rebirth of Archigram's ideals. The blob has come of age.

Simultaneously, a new batch of flying saucers, rockets and shuttles have been wheeled out onto urban launch pads, by architects seemingly harking back to an even older vision of the future, as espoused by Norman Bel Geddes in his 'Futurama'

display created for the 1939 New York World's Fair. 'Futurama' was a miniature plasterboard world of streamlined buildings and suburban rocket ports, over which floated airship hangars, in skies crossed by commuters' vapour trails. But this modern incarnation is more than paint and plaster, more than stage lighting and wobbly walls. This is science-fiction architecture that effortlessly flexes its mechanical muscles under smooth, ballistic skins, carefully sculpted using the latest in design and fabrication technology. Instead of shaky 'Doctor Who' sets, we see the production values of a Hollywood blockbuster.

Now that the true potential of the industrial world has been brought to bear on the building industry, we are left asking to what end this expertise should be used.

Do these buildings really offer any benefits over more conventional forms, or is the whole exercise one of showmanship, of headline-grabbing landmarks eager to become instant icons? Can these forms ever really be justified in practical terms, or are they a belated attempt at nostalgia by architects trying to recapture their 1960s dreams? By exploring each building in turn, we see if the technology they employ, and sometimes pioneer, make them prototypes that could transport us over a new architectural horizon.

To paraphrase John F. Kennedy, the architects choose to do these things not because they are easy, but because they are hard. As long as they keep pushing the technology to its limits, then the moon landing's magic will refuse to die.

Of all the famous Modern Movement architects that helped shaped the twentieth century, it is Oscar Niemeyer who has enjoyed the greatest longevity. His career spanning over sixty years, and with more than 500 buildings to his credit, Niemeyer has exerted a powerful architectural influence over his native Brazil from his studio in Rio. It is across the Guanabara Bay, just a ferry ride away, that Niemeyer created yet another tour de force in his quest for sculptural purity – not bad for a man then well into his nineties. The Museum of Contemporary Art or MAC (Museu de Arte Contemporânea) in Niterói stands poised on a peninsula surveying the bay. The need for the museum arose in 1991 when one of the most prominent art collectors in Brazil, João Sattamini, offered to loan his personal collection of Brazilian contemporary art to the city on the proviso that it was built a suitable home.

Niemeyer's response to the brief represents perhaps the clearest embodiment of his vision of Modernism in the twenty-first century: part machined aerodynamic component, part organic sculpture. Afforded a rocky promontory more usually reserved for lighthouses, the MAC is a beacon of culture, intent on luring visitors onto the rocks. The elegant form gives it a faintly retro-1960s air, the single column echoing the iconic fibreglass tulip chairs of Eero Saarrinen, and the Dan Dare comicbook illustrations of flying saucers from Mars. The architect himself uses a more organic point of reference: a flower, seemingly

MAC (MUSEU DE ARTE CONTEMPORANEA)

Up close, the aeronautical aspect of the façade becomes apparent, as it hovers above its cooling reflective pool.

ARCHITECT	Oscar Niemeyer
LOCATION	Niterói, Rio de Janeiro Brazil
LAUNCHED	1991–96

nourished by the pool beneath, rising out of the land on its broad stem. That stem, some 9 m (30 ft) thick, supports the flowering structure as it blooms to 16 m (52 ft) high and almost 50 m (164 ft) across. Niemeyer's strategy allows the gallery to take advantage of the drama of the setting and stand at the very edge of the narrow peninsula by virtue of its small footprint. The deceptively simple cantilevered form is only made possible thanks to the accomplished reinforced concrete structure, engineered by Niemeyer's long-time collaborator Bruno Contarini. The saucer itself is divided into three floors, with a further level partly sunken into the rock beneath the pool. The crisp, white-painted concrete of the swelling stem forms a canvas for the dancing sunlight reflected in the water below, animating its surface.

The gallery is ringed with a band of one-way tinted glass, gleaming jet-black like a visor on a crash helmet, and adding a slight air of menace (or at least uncertainty) as to what or whom is staring back out as you make your approach along the red, rendered spiral ramp. This sinuous twisting ribbon touches the building twice, looping back to allow access to the two upper levels. The slanting 40-degree sides of the saucer mean that the windows face downwards, protected by the 'peak' of the rim extending above, so avoiding the glare of the sun and affording visitors a view directly down onto the surf breaking on the rocks beneath.

Curved galleries often pose a problem when it comes to displaying their treasures. Frank Lloyd Wright's Guggenheim New York (1959) famously takes the form of a descending spiral ramp, exasperating its curators. Niemeyer neatly avoided such impracticalities by creating a hollow hexagon of partition walls around the centre, allowing works to be hung on both sides, but leaving the panorama of the bay uninterrupted. By providing gaps between the ends of the panels, visitors inside the hexagon are treated to tantalizing glimpses of the landscape beyond, giving the impression that nature is secretly trying to upstage the art.

In the latter stages of his career, Niemeyer's solutions seem to offer that magical formula of providing show-stopping icons with a practical purpose. The Museu de Arte Contemporânea, far from being simply a late flowering bloom by a venerable talent, is another chapter in a long career that has helped keep alive the vibrancy and inventiveness at the core of the Modern Movement.

The exposed location adds an element of pure drama, the gallery silhouetted against the mountain landscape of the bay, as if it is ready to launch off towards the city.

The highly pigmented ramps swirl out of the building like a futuristic red carpet enticing honoured guests towards the galleries.

The 360-degree viewing windows provide vertigo-inducing views of the rocky beach below, while catching the light reflected off the sea to illuminate the art.

So much has been written in open hostility about the Millennium Dome that it must be the most maligned structure in British architectural history. An ill-defined idea for the greatest millennium celebration on Earth, born under one government and continued by another not wishing to be seen as less aspiring, the Dome was a prime example of a starship without a real captain at the bridge. But if you step back from the PR disaster, and look at the overall structure that Richard Rogers and Buro Happold created, you have to marvel at the sheer scale and audacity of the project.

Given the time and budget available, the Dome's tent was the only cost-efficient structural solution that could cover a sufficiently large area and still be capable of meeting the deadline. The circumstances seem uncannily similar to the predicament faced by the Royal Commissioners of the Great Exhibition in 1850. With less than a year to the planned opening in May 1851, only Joseph Paxton's revolutionary prefabricated glass and cast iron structure offered the light and speedy solution required. Based on his own glasshouse designs and seemingly driven by the zeitgeist, Paxton erected a building six times the size of St Paul's Cathedral in just twenty-two weeks and created what many architects,

MILLENNIUM DOME

A bristling alien probe, the dome spent its life under a cloud but was the only element of the whole project that came in on time and on budget. Illuminated at night the translucent skin glowed from within thanks to the lighting arrangement by Imagination.

ARCHITECT	Richard Rogers Partnership
LOCATION	Greenwich, London, England
CREATED	1996–98

including Richard Rogers, consider to be the world's first modern building, the Crystal Palace.

Whereas Paxton's creation was always intended to be dismantled, the Dome's building schedule was thrown into disarray by a conceptual U-turn. The original decision to opt for a PVC-coated polyester roof fabric – an option approximately £8 million cheaper than more durable PTFE-coated glassfibre – was overturned in the face of a public outcry at the ballooning costs of a very temporary exhibition. With the political sands shifting to calm public opinion, the move was made to give the Dome greater longevity, by opting for the PTFE alternative, which would have a lifespan of at least twenty-five years. Several months of design work had to be scrapped and the job of detailing the fabric had to begin afresh. All of the components were redesigned from scratch, including the two-piece aluminium extrusion clamps, 25,000 of which are used to secure the 144 separate flat fabric panels to the web of cables. These panels total 100,000 m² (1 million sq ft) of tensioned fabric, which, thanks to the underlying structure, is capable of supporting the weight of a jumbo jet even though the skin itself is only 1 mm ($^1/_{32}$ in.) thick.

The structure's dimensions alone put it into the 'super' league. The largest fabric structure in the world standing 50 m (164 ft) high at its centre, and 320 m (1,050 ft) in diameter, it encloses 80,000 m² (861,000 ft²) of exhibition space. Perhaps the biggest misnomer about the Millennium Dome is its name. Structurally speaking, it isn't a dome at all, as the canopy is not a ridged element, but a complex web of cables under tension hung off yet more cables under tension. The whole building is effectively pulling itself out of the ground, with the twelve 100 m (328 ft) long cigar-shaped masts, each weighing 105 tons (95 tonnes), suspended in the web of cables. Small wonder then, that the twenty-four reinforced concrete anchors around the circumference extend 24 m (79 ft) into the ground. The crane required to lift these masts into position was so large that it took twenty-four lorries just to bring it onto site.

Multiples of twelve appear frequently in the Dome's statistics, and the repetitive nature of the structure meant that assembly on site speeded up considerably as the contractors raised one identical element after, becoming faster each time. From the first of the 5,000 piles being driven into the peninsula till the moment the Dome 'topped out' on June 22 1998 took exactly a year and a day. The result remains the largest fabric-covered structure in the world. Paxton would have been impressed. Large enough to be visible from space and with its purity of form and direct sense of purpose, the architecture of aspiration has never looked bigger.

Twelve steel-finned cylinders around the circumference of the dome act as containers for the plant and services. Part of Rogers's well-practiced strategy to leave interiors as uncluttered as possible, their exposed working parts are theatrically lit to add to the drama.

A finely spun web of cables forms the central hub, reflecting the Dome's dominant design principle of 'high redundancy'. If one cable fails, there are always six others to take the load. The delicate cable system was tested with a computer program called 'Tensyl', developed by Buro Happold over twenty years.

It is only when the swarms of construction workers abseil into shot that the massive size of the bright yellow masts becomes apparent.

NATWEST MEDIA CENTRE

Cricket is not a sport renowned for its love of change. The Marylebone Cricket Club (MCC) is still, in the twenty-first century, an august institution composed almost entirely of men who would look askance at the thought of players being allowed to wear shorts, let alone drinking coffee instead of tea. But a visitor to Lord's Cricket Ground will only have to turn their gaze momentarily from the steady thump of leather on willow to see that the MCC is perhaps not as reactionary as it might first appear. For above the crowds of portly, sunburnt supporters in floppy hats, there hovers something far sleeker and infinitely more refined.

The NatWest Media Centre at Lord's is one of the truly iconic buildings within the sporting world. As though controlling things from the bridge of the 'S. S. Enterprise', cricket commentators survey the ground laid out before them, seemingly judging their approach speed prior to landing on the batsman's crease. The stand's elliptical profile, with the relatively flat top and bottom, encompasses a semi-monocoque structure in which the shell does not actually bear its own weight. Beneath the smooth aluminium skin, lies a wealth of welded struts and beams similar to the plank construction of frame ships. This is no coincidence as the entire structure was prefabricated in strips up to 3 m (10 ft) wide in a Dutch boatyard and then transported to site for final assembly. The sections were then hoisted into place and seam-welded before being waterproofed. The shell has no expansion joints so the final white coating was necessary in order to keep heat expansion within workable limits, as well as contributing to the overall 'Star Trek' feel of the structure.

ARCHITECT	Future Systems
LOCATION	Lord's Cricket Ground, London, England
CREATED	1994–99

Left: From front or back, the Media stand is equally dynamic, leaving the viewer uncertain of its direction of travel. The hollow legs are only partially covered in GRP panels, allowing breezes to cool the wheezing pundits as they rush to their seats.

Right: The glossy white shell of the Media Centre, contrasts with the gaping black mouth of its fully glazed façade, shaded from the sun by the lean of its brow.

The stand rests on two 12 m (39 ft) legs that are supported on tension piles extending 26 m (85 ft) into the ground. The steel staircase that provides access to the viewing deck also acts as a structural element, cross-bracing the legs from within. The stand's main shell is 40 m (131 ft) long and 20 m (66 ft) deep. Inside the crisp, white carapace is a spacious double-tiered interior that can accommodate over 200 journalists and broadcasters, providing them with superb views of the day's play. As you would expect of such a futuristic facility, the pundits have access to the best information and communication technology available, not to mention cream teas and scones. Behind them are all the meeting rooms, bars and conveniences necessary keep the sporting press at the coal-face.

As it floats above the ground it is hard to decide whether its graceful form is more akin to a luxury yacht or a B-29's fuselage, or perhaps even the carefully sculpted air intake on a handmade Bentley's bonnet. (The latter reference is more likely to have caught the imagination of the committee members of the MCC.) It is one of the few buildings that looks exactly like the futuristic computer-generated images that architects show to their potential clients, but then Future Systems are well-named.

Partners Jan Kaplicky and Amanda Levete have a long history of producing advanced building designs that utilize materials and techniques from other industries, but Lord's represented their first large-scale commission. The stand is the world's first all-aluminium building, bringing established boatbuilding methods to the conservative construction trade. The architects, along with project engineers Ove Arup, had to fight hard to persuade the client to go with this method rather than use a steel structure, skinned in aluminium plates. In their quest to prove the semi-monocoque viable they consulted Falmouth-based boatbuilder, Pendennis, using one of their 35 m (115 ft) motor cruisers as a costing guide. Their efforts paid off, and the completed structure with its smooth, uncluttered aluminium exterior wooed the judges of the prestigious Stirling Prize for Architecture in 1999.

This is the architecture of a future where technology is hidden beneath a flawless skin; a world of gleaming corridors echoing with the quiet hum of machinery and the near-silent hiss of sliding airlock doors. Captain James T. Kirk would feel at home watching the Ashes from such a vantage point, though perhaps Commander Spock might not be so at ease. 'Captain, surely taking five days to complete a single game is not logical?'

Rising at the join between the curved sweep of the Compton and Edrich stands, the Media centre pokes up like a periscope over the spectators' heads.

Above: The toughened, laminated glass screen through which the commentators gaze is inclined at twenty-five degrees to ensure that reflections from the sun do not blind the players they are so studiously observing.

Left: Four racked lines of seats line the front of each tier of the building, ensuring that every cricket hack is afforded an interrupted view of the ground laid out before them.

SPAARNE HOSPITAL
BUS STATION

Though by no means the largest building in this survey, the Spaarne Hospital Bus station still manages to find its way into the record books as the world's biggest structure built entirely from synthetic materials: factory-cut polystyrene blocks, covered with a spray-on polyester skin. The limited budget (1 million euros) necessitated this choice of material, as the more expensive poured concrete would have required complicated on-site shuttering and skilled labour. Computer Numeric Control (CNC) cutters were used to realize the form, which was made in five sections before being moved to site for assembly. The ultra-light polystyrene was glued together, then anchored to the concrete base by bolts,

ARCHITECT	NIO Architecten
LOCATION	Hoofddorp, Netherlands
CREATED	2003

Viewed through the green structural loop, the bus looks like it has been swallowed whole by the hungry whale.

before a final spray coating of polyester was applied to give a uniform finish.

The architects have skilfully combined all the necessary elements of a bus station into a single free-flowing form. Seating, passenger toilets and litterbins are all recessed directly into pre-cut cavities in the polystyrene, while the loop of the roof provides shelter for passengers embarking from either side. At the west end of the structure, the architects have even carved out a small rest facility for the drivers. The structure does raise questions about how sophisticated design software, combined with techniques usually reserved for rapid prototyping, could radically alter the face of architecture in the future. These methods make for almost instant buildings that only reveal their true dimensions when assembled on site. The bus station itself is an impressive 50 m long, 10 m wide and 5 m high (164 x 33 x 16 ft). The structure's ingenuity was duly recognized by the 'Architectural Review', who awarded it an ar+d prize in 2003.

The structure's unconventional shape has encouraged commentators to use a wide variety of analogies in an attempt to name its aesthetic. The word 'blob' comes up quite frequently. The architects, NIO Architecten, seem open to all these interpretations ('eroded boulder', 'random self-generated form',

'Henry Mooresque sculpture'), but they themselves refer to it as 'The Amazing Whale Jaw'. Marooned on its concrete traffic island, the bus station does have the appearance of the beached remains of a large sea mammal, stripped down to sun-bleached bone. But the concrete base acts almost like a plinth, reinforcing the idea that this is a one-off piece of sculpture intended to be viewed and considered. What patients emerging from the hospital after artificial hip replacements make of it is another matter.

Prior to establishing NIO Architecten in 2000, Maurice Nio spent much of the 1990s working with BDG Architekten Ingenieurs on the AVI-Twente Waste Incineration Plant, Hengelo (1993–97). For him, at least, the bus station must represent a pleasing role-reversal, exploiting the full potential of a material that more usually finds itself burnt or discarded in landfill sites. The architects claim to have thoroughly tested their unconventional material and are confident that the structure will have a long life, resisting the daily routine of abuse – knives, graffiti and cigarette burns – meted out to street furniture. The slightly unsettling truth is that the self-coloured material has quietly begun a gradual change, as a green pigment emerges from the once-yellow polyester. It is as though the building, chameleon-like, is slowly, organically morphing of its own accord leading the nervous observer to wonder if, perhaps, the bus station has future plans of its own...

Top right: The cabin at one end provides the bus drivers with the opportunity for quiet relaxation, well insulated against traffic noise by the thickness of the polystyrene, no doubt quite oblivious to the fact that they have been packaged like so many white goods.

Bottom right: The fat bulbous form, like a muscular boa constrictor, is already beginning to show the lurid green mottling that is oozing through the skin.

The underbelly of the beast, with its recessed fluorescent tubes, does not present a particularly comforting aspect to the waiting passengers, but does afford them shelter.

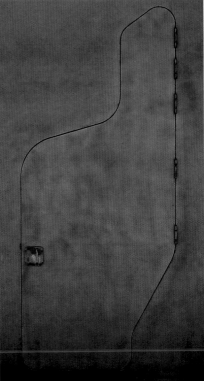

The door to the drivers' cabin has a profile as unconventional as the form into which it is set, suggesting that it was intended for occupants with a distinctly alien body form.

On arriving at the Eden Project, you might be forgiven for thinking that you've stumbled upon a human colony clustered for survival on an inhospitable planet in a far-flung galaxy. Nestling in the crater of a former china clay pit, like a sprawling mass of soap bubbles, the Eden project's eight interlinking forms take on the appearance of a subterranean creature slowing oozing out of the ground.

The original plan to create a giant glasshouse, in the mould of Joseph Paxton's Crystal Palace, was quickly dropped due to the unstable site. Wet clay slowly dries and cracks, altering ground levels in far greater increments than glass tolerances would stand. Instead, the final scheme fulfils the vision of structural engineer, Richard Buckminster Fuller, whose geodesic dome system (patented in 1954) articulated his quest to enclose the maximum volume within a minimal surface area, using the least material. Fuller's work has been a strong influence on the generation of British architects who developed the High-Tech style. Along with Foster and Rogers, Eden's architect Nicholas Grimshaw has always made reference to Fuller's theories in his own work. Grimshaw came to the project after completing the successful Eurostar Terminal at Waterloo (1992–94), another structural exercise in light and transparency over large spans.

The completed structure was the result of a close collaboration between the architects, the engineers Anthony Hunt & Partners, and the project's founder Tim Smit. In Smit's own words, their 'interests lie in explaining how the natural world works, seen through the lens of plants, exploring how people might best organize themselves in the face of this knowledge and thereby reach an understanding of what sustainability might mean and, through best practice of these principles, create an organization that is sustainable to act as a model for others.' The complex is divided into two main 'biomes', or climate zones, specifically chosen to show the diversity of plant life on earth: the Humid Tropics (rainforests and tropical islands), and the Warm and Temperate Regions (Mediterranean, South African and Californian). Cornwall's own temperate climate has led the project leaders to refer to the surrounding landscape as the 'Outdoor Biome', reflecting the surprisingly wide variety of plant life that thrives there, including specimens from as far afield as India.

Left: All the biomes' components conform to the ridged hexagonal grid, including the dramatic entrances that incorporate mechanical air intakes, drawing both visitors and air into the cavernous interior.

Right: Sheltered from cooling winds by the high sides of the china clay pit, the shiny self-cleaning surface of the biomes reflects the play of clouds as they breeze by overhead.

THE EDEN PROJECT

ARCHITECT	Nicholas Grimshaw & Partners
LOCATION	St Austell, Cornwall England
CREATED	1995–2001

These are truly massive structures, the largest conservatories in the world, with the Humid Tropics Biome at 240 m (287 ft) long and 110 m (361 ft) wide, boasting a maximum internal height of 55 m (180 ft). The underlying geometry of the biomes is based on giant spheres, with their invisible projected centres all sharing the same common depth below ground level, following a rough S-shaped line. The hexagonal modular components vary in size between the 'biomes' with the largest ones almost 11 m (36 ft) across. The structure is double-layered, with the outer formed of hexagonal steel components, with each corner resting on a triangular pyramid whose lower edges join to form a second layer of hexagons, rotated at 30 degrees. This repetitive modular structure was self-supporting, removing the need for scaffolding during construction.

Instead of glass, pneumatic pillows of ETFE (a polymer of ethylene and tetrafluoroethylene) foil, zipped into hexagonal modules, were employed to form the light and flexible structure. Air pumps keep the pillows inflated and the trapped air between the triple layers of ETFE acts as insulation. ETFE itself is a remarkably space-age material; it is only 1 per cent of the weight of glass, and, in triple-layer form, it has the insulation properties of double-glazing. It is also highly transparent to a wide spectrum of light, and this, combined with careful siting by computer-driven solar modelling, allows Eden to utilize the optimum solar gain throughout the year. It is also strong, anti-static and extremely smooth, making it practically self-cleaning. At the end of its anticipated life span – in excess of forty years – ETFE's biodegradable properties will further contribute to the 'green' ethos at the heart of the project. The biomes themselves are a model of sustainability, with rainwater being recycled for humidification and the ground water seepage used for irrigation.

Eden represents man's attempt to control his own environment, and to study and understand its mechanisms. It could well also prove to be a useful prototype, should the predicted climate changes make the Earth a much less hospitable place.

Left: The sight of two workers busily checking one of the connecting nodes, like ants swarming over a fallen fruit, gives some indicator of the biomes' massive scale.

Above: The climactic controls the biomes offer mean that visitors to Cornwall can meander through the jungles of an almost prehistoric landscape, even in the depths of winter.

Right: Soaring over the lush green tropical landscape, the apex of each biome is crowned with a cluster of five subdivided modules, which house the triangular mechanical louvres that control the internal temperature.

THE SAGE

Like Birmingham, Newcastle upon Tyne has felt the long drawn-out effects of manufacturing decline, with its once-proud engineering and shipbuilding industries all but spent. As part of the regeneration of the Newcastle quayside, a competition was launched in 1997 for the design of a world-class concert hall to complement other on-going initiatives that included the conversion of the Baltic Flour Mills into a contemporary art gallery. Foster & Partners' scheme, comprising three auditoriums, a music education centre and all the associated plant under a single swooping canopy, won the competition. The lines of the dramatic canopy were partly inspired by the sweeping curves of the neighbouring Tyne bridges that have long been the city's visual signature, while the project's name was decided by the £6 million donation made by the Newcastle software company, Sage Group Plc.

The building occupies a steeply sloping site at the river's edge, with a road running immediately in front of the façade. The canopy acts as an additional layer of sound insulation against traffic noise and has entrances at both ends to form a raised covered concourse populated with cafés and bars open to the public sixteen hours a day. This concept of routes through buildings to encourage their development as social hubs is a recurring theme in Foster's recent work and had been successfully applied at the Great Court in the British Museum in London (2000). The area

Left: At night the Sage sits glowing by the riverside, framed by Wilkinson Eyre's 'blinking' Millennium Bridge whose lines also resonate with the older Tyne bridges. With the Baltic Art Gallery, they form a trio of recent additions, the focus of the area's regeneration.

Right: From across the river, the Sage looks like a wave of rolling, glittering surf about to crash down the bank into the Tyne, its pixilated skin reflecting a myriad of sky tones.

ARCHITECT	Foster & Partners
LOCATION	Gateshead, Tyne & Wear, England
CREATED	1997–2004

enclosed by the 'shrink-wrapped' roof also functions as a circulation space between the auditoriums. Performers can rub shoulders with their audiences on the way to the stage, creating a greater air of informality in keeping with the inclusive nature of the venue. The concrete slab floor is the only component that touches each of the six elements (three halls and three plant units) within the complex. This level of isolation was necessary to prevent noise from the services reaching the performance spaces, or a performance in one hall interfering with another.

The Sage is in some ways deceptively futuristic, with the elegant curving roof simply cocooning the separate elements in a single public space with a unified outward appearance. Like the bonnet of a high-performance car cloaking its engine, the roof's graceful curves follow the contours of the halls beneath. This gives the shell-like structure a cleaner, more distinctive profile on the cityscape than a cluster of smaller structures would have had. The streamlining also helps channel the prevailing wind, encouraging air to circulate around the concourse.

Buro Happold engineered the roof structure, which covers a span of 80 m (262 ft). The four main steel arches, linked horizontally by steel members, support the cladding of 3,000 linen-finish stainless-steel panels, while a further 280 glass panels have been used to give views out over the Tyne and bring natural light into the interiors. All the panels are flat, and this pixilated geometric composition, with the constantly changing angles, makes for a far more interesting play of light over the roof's surface than a curved panel system would have provided. To reduce construction costs, the roof's surface was kept to a minimum and the whole structure has a lean efficiency, in sharp contrast to the more sculptural approach taken by Gehry's Guggenheim Bilbao (1997). The money that might have been spent on superfluous cladding went into providing the highly versatile and acoustically excellent performance spaces, which are so carefully designed that they can be tuned to suit different styles of music, broadening the venue's appeal to the widest spectrum of tastes.

The Sage is a sleek, futuristic landmark building where practicality has not being sacrificed in pursuit of looks. This well-considered combination of appropriate form and logical layout is typical of Foster & Partners's work, and reinforces their position as one the most successful architectural practices in the world.

Approached from the rear, the Sage suddenly appears over the horizon, like an immense metallic caterpillar slinking towards the bridge.

Opposite, top left: The streamlined cantilevered concrete balconies providing access to the internal seating are dramatically lit at night, enticing visitors into the interior.

Opposite, top right: The concrete-floored concourse of the circulation space follows the contours of the undulating façade, providing a convenient sheltered vantage point from which to watch the river traffic.

Right: The exterior streamlined balconies correspond to the tiers of seating inside the main auditorium, a warm glowing space of ribbed ash walls with natural birch seats and balustrades.

Birmingham, the city that once laid claim to being 'the workshop of the world', fell on hard times in the post-war manufacturing slump and this, combined with some soulless town-planning in the 1960s, gave the second largest city in the UK something of an edifice complex. But the 1990s saw its famous Jewellery Quarter and large public squares being repaved and filled with modern sculpture, and a slow revival of its commercial centre. The canal system, the arteries of the old industrial heartland, also played its part in providing a tranquil element to developments such as Brindley Place, which acts as a centre for exhibitions and business events by day, and thriving bar- and club-land at night.

Into this bubbling mixture of rebuilding and regeneration, Future Systems have dropped a retail bombshell. The new Selfridges department store forms part of a development branded the 'Bullring', in a reference to the dilapidated 1964 covered shopping centre that was demolished to give a more coherent, pedestrian-oriented shopping district. Selfridges' blue biomorphic form, studded with almost 15,000 anodized aluminium discs, blinks in the sun like an enormous fly's eye greedily surveying the hordes of shoppers that pass under its nose. This Martian store squats on a corner site opposite the fourteenth-century, Gothic-style spire of St Martin's church, as if preparing to slowly ooze over and envelope this last fragment of the area's original architecture, in an act vaguely symbolic of old-time religion's ousting by the gods of mass consumerism.

The undulating, curvaceous form was achieved by using a flexible expanded metal mesh, hung from the building's steel framework in storey-height ribbons like rock strata, which was

SELFRIDGES

At night the silver-studded behemoth sits silent, its upper window glowing like a Cyclops's eye, waiting to spend another day devouring the constant stream of shoppers that pour through the curving, glazed footbridge from the carpark.

ARCHITECT	Future Systems
LOCATION	Birmingham, England
CREATED	1999–2003

sprayed with a 17.5 cm (7 in.) concrete render to form a hard shell. Over this went a further 7.5 cm (3 in.) layer of mineral fibre insulation, painted with a liquid waterproof membrane that was topped with a unifying final skin of acrylic render. The blue colour of the skin was inspired by the work of the artist Yves Klein, whose 1950s work explores the creation of voids on a flat surface. It was this visual 'depth' that the architects were striving to emulate, as they needed to find a way to articulate what would have otherwise been a very large and uninviting blank canvas. The colour itself was produced using Monolastex, a product made by Liquid Plastics, which is more commonly used to paint lighthouses. Designed to withstand the violent abrasion of the sea, the finish is extremely resilient, with a predicted lifespan of thirty-five years without fading or deterioration, certainly long enough for this building to make waves of its own.

In order to provide flexible cladding for their big blue blob, the architects had to design a modular system capable of being moulded around the curves they'd created. The choice of discs rather than triangles (which are the preferred building blocks of architects such as Foster & Partners) gives Selfridges the retro-pop aesthetic of the 1960s, as opposed to high-tech futurism. Inspiration is also said to have come from the shimmering chain-mail dresses of designer Paco Rabanne, transforming the building into precisely the kind of fashion statement that Selfridges's commissioning executive Vittorio Radice was seeking in order to entice a fresh young clientele through the doors. The discs themselves are 660 mm (26 in.) in diameter and made from pressed and spun aluminium sheet that was polished to a mirror finish before being anodized. They were then attached by hand to the rendered façade using stainless-steel rods, their cupped inner faces pressed against the walls and sealed by foam ring gaskets to prevent moisture penetrating the joints. The junctions between the end of the disc pattern and the glazing at street level are cunningly disguised by projecting the windows out from the building's surface and allowing the discs to run behind their opaque yellow rebates. Behind the glass, pressed aluminium drainage channels catch the run-off, and discretely pipe it away.

Perhaps most remarkable thing about this building, is the fact that Future Systems were able to deliver this commercial coup d'état within the same budget as the more everyday Debenham's store opposite. For an architectural practice that spent years planning but rarely finding a client brave enough to build, Selfridges has marked a coming of age. Or rather, a return to an age where spacecraft came in saucer form.

Opposite: Accessed from balconies and bridges at various levels, the entrances to the sheer studded faces of the building are all framed by yellow-backed glass halos that contrast with the blue of the façade's render.

Left: The sloping sides and increasing diameters of the floor apertures create a tapered central atrium that allows sunlight to penetrate deep into the interior, reflecting off the smooth curves of the escalators.

Above: The futuristic halo to the escalators was created with a combination of fibreglass and glass-reinforced plaster cladding, which morphs organically into the ceiling.

KUNSTHAUS GRAZ

ARCHITECT	Spacelab – Peter Cook & Colin Fournier
LOCATION	Graz, Austria
CREATED	2001–03

While the world's of music and contemporary art were undergoing a revolution in the swinging 1960s, the British architectural profession seemed stuck in the past, turning out bland interpretations of pre-war Bauhaus modernism. From this professional malaise sprang Archigram, a group of young like-minded architects on a mission to shock the establishment out of its complacency and embrace the opportunities that modern technology could offer. Archigram began publishing a magazine in 1961 in which they expounded their radical new ideas. With their bright cartoon-strip montages, Ron Herron and Peter Cook

In this pastel-toned, Baroque town, the Kunsthaus is a wild card. Opened in time to form a focal point for Graz's stint as European City of Culture in 2003, the building has a basic concrete core with a steel frame, but is skinned with a 'membrane' of 2 x 3 m (6.5 x 10 ft) acrylic panels that sandwich 925 circular light fittings against the inner skin. The lights bring the alien to life, each one computer-controlled to transform the skin into a media façade, a giant monochrome communications device, beaming its messages across the city in sophisticated pulsing patterns, images or text. The skin and underlying steel structure were designed using software intended for boatbuilding and the science of fluid dynamics has evidently been absorbed to create a flowing biomorphic organism, with lights throbbing as if it had a heartbeat. By day the most distinctive features are the sixteen nozzles that protrude from the alien's back, facing north to draw light into the interior. The light drawn in by the nozzles often proves insufficient to illuminate the exhibition space so dramatic concentric fluorescent tubes line the apertures, giving them the effect of teleportation devices ready to abduct unwary visitors. The architects ran into problems almost straight away with some of their more fanciful ideas, such as reactive rubberized nozzles, and a translucent skin, being vetoed on the grounds of cost. Ironically, in order to meet its share of the funding for the friendly

Left: From across the river Mur, the Kunsthaus rises out of its nest of trees, the sixteen alien nozzles straining upwards like the heads of hungry expectant chicks.

Right: The mass of the building seems about to envelope the surrounding buildings with the clearance between them as little as 2 m (6.5 ft) in places. Given the awkward shape of the site, the organic form offered the best way to maximize the building's volume.

offered a lively and optimistic antidote to the stale architectural scene. Despite being acclaimed as one of the most influential movements in post-war architecture, the small group of architects, that later included Colin Fournier, split up in 1974 having never completed a major scheme. It is only in the twenty-first century that Cook and Fournier's vision of the future has finally been given physical form and the world is now able to assess a train of thought that had been sitting in a quiet siding for thirty years. The result? The world's largest space cucumber, a 'friendly alien' that has landed in the quiet city of Graz.

alien, the city of Graz was obliged to sell off the airport runway.
Final costs came to £27 million, only 3 per cent over budget.

The 'needle', the lozenge-shaped structure perched on the side
of the building, was another victim of cost-cutting and practicality.
It was meant to be a rooftop restaurant, but there was no way of
providing a fire escape from the kitchen so the hungry 'blob' had
to go unfed. The needle now functions as a viewing platform, a
light space compared to the slightly dingy galleries, and a physical
connection, like a docking rig, to the neighbouring Eiernes Haus.

The whole building, though both sculptural and visually
stimulating, clearly illustrates how space-age aesthetics can be
brought back to earth by the realities of budget and building
regulations. In purely practical terms, the signature skin may
also prove to be more of a curse than a blessing, as what was
envisaged as a slick, seamless shell (as embodied by the NatWest
Media Centre) has become a patchwork quilt of widely spaced
panels to allow for expansion joints. Despite the precautions of
heated gutters and snow-catchers, large lumps of snow and ice
soon collect under the skin next to the electronics. The fact that
the bulbs can only be changed by hinging the panels forward from
the outside makes maintaining the building a tricky business.
'Sustainable' is unlikely to be a term much used in conjunction
with the Kunsthaus, but its sense of 'fun' is a blast from
Archigram's swinging past.

The lights, or BIX (the term coined by
their designers at Realities: United by
combining 'big' and 'pixel'), transform
the skin at night, making it pulse like a
living organism.

Right: Like a gigantic pumpkin hollowed
out to become a Halloween lantern, the
Kunsthaus's upper galleries follow the
curving skin, the steel ceiling panels
punctured by the nozzle skylights with
their glowing rings of fluorescent light.

When Norman Foster's Swiss RE Headquarters building was completed in 2004, it became an instant icon, part of the city's lexicon of landmarks, and as much part of London's skyline as St Paul's and Tower Bridge. It was also the first major skyscraper to have been built in the City of London in over thirty years, marking a shift in attitudes towards high-rise development that had not been seen in the capital since the early 1980s. Before Swiss RE, the most radical structure to rise out of the financial district had been Richard Rogers's Lloyd's Building, and the difference between them shows how far British High-Tech architecture has come in the intervening years. This is no blocky Miesian monolith to be reviled, but a sleek, shining rocket, ready to blast off from the Square Mile.

The complex engineering calculations necessary to generate the exterior geometry were performed using parametric modelling software originally developed in the automotive and aerospace industries for designing the complex curves of fuselage and bodywork. These programs allow architects to experiment with different forms by mapping relationships between components, rather than simply acting as digital version of conventional drawings. When the designer changes one element, the linked components automatically adjust to the alteration, making a significant time-saving. This enables the design to be more adventurous, and more thoroughly tested, with any alternatives explored well before work begins on site.

But it is not so much the use of computer-aided design that makes Swiss RE so significant, as the emphasis on sustainability and energy efficiency. A tall building is inherently greedy when it comes to power consumption compared to a lower-rise counterpart of an equivalent volume. Much more energy is needed to power lifts, raise water, and circulate air over multiple levels and, at 180 m (590 ft) tall, with forty-one floors, Swiss RE has

SWISS RE

ARCHITECTS	Foster & Partners
LOCATION	30 St Mary Axe, London, England
CREATED	1997–2004

Far left: The gracefully curving bands of contrasting clear and tinted glass imbue the building with an almost Art Deco air, but are an outward expression of the tower's innovative plan, rather than being purely decorative.

Left: At the main entrance from the plaza the diagonal grid of the main structural beams is left unglazed to create an open double-height entrance hall, a triumphal geometric portal through which all visitors must pass.

Right: The voluptuous curves and striking façade mean that the tower presents an equally attractive face from whatever direction it is viewed. Instantly recognizable, it has taken its place among more venerable landmarks on London's skyline.

Spiralling voids are created by the
twisted floorplans that swirl up through
the building like turbine blades, helping
power the natural ventilation system.

all of these needs. However, with this radical new form, Foster's office have sought to cut the amount of energy required to an estimated 50 per cent of that used by a conventional tower block. Their strategy relies on minimizing the need for air conditioning and artificial lighting by encouraging natural convection and creating a transparent façade. The diagonally braced outer structure, divided into triangles like a massive space-frame, supports the building's weight, allowing for column-free interior plans. Unlike the Lloyd's building, the majority of the exterior glazing is clear, allowing natural light to penetrate directly into the interior, and providing views out to the city.

The floorplans themselves are like rectangular fingers radiating from the centre of the circular cross-section, leaving six triangular voids around the circumference. The floor plan rotates as it rises, leaving each floor's voids to form spiralling grooves that twist to a point near the apex. These are the building's lungs, using natural convection to draw air in at ground level and through computer-controlled vents in the grooves, spinning it up through the building as it warms.

The tower's bullet shape tapers at both top and bottom, giving more public space in the square below while creating pressure differentials that further help drive the air circulation. The aerodynamic form also benefits pedestrians in the square below as wind flows around the building, whereas a flat façade would have created uncomfortably strong downdrafts. Swiss RE's reward for being prepared to back this radical form can be found in the 'nose cone' which houses a restaurant for the occupants and their clients. From this column-free vantage point, diners can enjoy possibly the finest views in London.

In recognition of the project's advanced ecological agenda, and status as the first 'green' office block in London, Foster & Partners were awarded the prestigious RIBA Stirling Prize in 2004. Swiss RE heralds a new age for skyscraper design, beginning a worldwide trend for streamlined bullet forms that looks set to take hold both in Europe and the Far East.

Above: The delicate lattice of the restaurant canopy offers diners uninterrupted 360-degree views across London and is possibly the best corporate incentive Swiss RE could offer its clients.

Right: The bullet nose of Swiss RE stands out defiantly against the angular edges of its predecessors at Canary Wharf that now appear to be huddling nervously at a safe distance.

In surveying over fifty years of man's attempts to build the future, it seems that we have come full circle. With the advent of computer-aided design, the shapes and forms of the 1950s and 1960s comicbooks have become viable propositions, and architects have seized the opportunity to create a range of buildings with a retro-aesthetic that was once confined to the realms of popular science-fiction.

In the varied projects presented here, we have seen many attempts to reinvigorate architecture and escape the mundanity of the modern world by creating visual interest, be it in the form, surface pattern, texture or colour. Any evaluation of such attempts should be subject to the same rigorous analysis that the structural or ergonomic elements of the building have to satisfy. A comparison between The Deep and Selfridges brings this debate into focus, for both buildings are effectively 'black boxes', almost windowless containers, one for aquatic life and the other for shoals of consumers. Both architects were faced with the prospect of having to articulate what would otherwise be a vast blank surface, devoid of expression, and find a language that would fit both context and function. Farrell's consummate exercise in architectural metaphors makes The Deep resonate on multiple levels, the underlying strands of his design being easily discernable to the casual observer. It is a futuristic building that knows where it came from and where it is going. For applied decoration to be successful, there needs to be this directness,

this tangibility. In many ways Selfridges posed Future Systems with a more difficult task, as it is not founded on the bedrock of history but on the shifting sands of the high street where it runs the risk of becoming as ephemeral as the chainmail gowns that were its inspiration. Fashions come and go and to tie a building to something so transient may prove to be the building's undoing in the long term. If The Deep is a landmark built to educate, to inform and to last, then Selfridges is a beautiful expensive bauble, rather than a priceless heirloom.

Having finally been given the opportunity to create one of their fantasy structures in Graz, Archigram's former members have produced a truly iconic building, but one that exposes the weaknesses in their visions of the future that their colourful montages could never convey. The world has waited so long for them to be realized that they already look like retro-throwbacks to the 1960s and the practical maintenance problems the building presents suggest that it could never be a model for a truly sustainable future. The muttered concerns for the environment that were only just being voiced in the 1960s have now grown to a clamour of real fears for the world in which we live. The sheltered dreams of Archigram's unbuilt schemes have grown stale while Foster and his contemporaries have been busily building all over the world and evolving a vocabulary that accounts for the realities that new materials and climate change have thrown at them. The reality of the Swiss RE outstrips the fantasy of the Kunsthaus. One seems destined to become the

CONCLUSION

prototype for much of high-rise building for the next decade, while the other is a glorious one-off, unlikely to be replicated.

In all likelihood, it is Foster's approach to energy-efficiency that will preoccupy architects well into the twenty-first century, for while low-tech solutions may provide answers for certain building types, only the advanced science of computer-predicted energy consumption can really turn the tide of city-dwelling in favour of eco-principles. The emergence of China as the next economic super-power, hungry for the physical trappings of the West, has led to an unparalleled building boom that threatens not only to erase its past, but additionally to create cripplingly unsustainable demands for energy to feed the skyscrapers hovering over their cities like vultures. It is in the Far East that the next battle of architectural ideology needs to be fought and won, for if the planet is not to run out of resources then surely the largest, most populous nation on earth must take up the baton offered in the form of Swiss RE. It is up to architects to provide them with sleek, seductive buildings that offer both the prestige but, more importantly, the sustainability that the world community as a whole needs to embrace.

The question remains as to what form the homes of the future will take. However seductive the bespoke sculpted curves of houses by Kellogg, Tsui and Prince, they can never fulfill the needs of an ever-growing world population. Must we contend with a future that finds us living in mass-produced prefabricated pods, like so many Lloyd's toilet cubicles stacked upon one another to

achieve the required densities? Maybe not. There could well be an alternative to the rectilinear piles of Peter Cook's Plug-In Cities and once again advanced engineering seems set to provide the panacea. Still in its infancy, 'Freeform' construction makes use of computer-controlled robotics inherited from the production lines of the automotive industries, adapting them from welding and spraying to extruding slip concrete and polymer materials. On frames erected over the building site, these robots can ride up and down while being constantly fed construction data from computer models. They literally 'print' buildings in consecutive layers like a three-dimensional fax, in the same way that rapid prototypes of cars or mobile phones are currently made from resin. At the push of a button, a design that has only existed in a virtual world can be fabricated over and over again, without hand ever touching trowel.

There are still some major technical obstacles to overcome, mainly relating to how the robots interpret the data, but if perfected, this technique could well change the way we build and design the world around us. With the cost of skilled labour removed, it could just as easily be harnessed to turn out miniature High Desert Houses as dry uniform boxes, offering the tantalizing prospect of bespoke homes for all. The 'Freeform' engineers may well have devised the ultimate tool with which architects can express their art in years to come.

Only one thing is for sure. The future's out there.

'More and more the engineering is becoming the only way that the artist in the architect can get his art expressed.'

Paul Westbury, Director, Buro Happold[5]

INDEX OF ARCHITECTS' WEBSITES

If you have been inspired by one or more of the projects featured in this book, then you may be interested to know that many of the architectural practices have excellent websites where you can find out more about their past work, personal histories and future projects.

PICTURE CREDITS

For further information about the work of the
photographers featured in this book go to:
www.arcaid.co.uk

SELECT BIBLIOGRAPHY

BOOKS

Able, Chris, **Sky High – Vertical Architecture**, Royal Academy Publications/Thames & Hudson, London, UK, 2003.

Campell-Lange, Barbara-Ann, **Lautner**, Taschen, Cologne, Germany, 2005

Colquhoun, Kate, **A Thing in Disguise – The Visionary Life of Joseph Paxton**, Harper Perennial, an imprint of Harper Collins, London, UK, 2004.

Costantino, Maria, **The Life and Works of Frank Lloyd Wright**, Courage Books/PRC Publishing, London, UK, 1998.

Crosbie, Michael J., **Curtain Walls: Recent Developments by Cesar Pelli & Associates**, Birkhäuser, Basel, Switzerland, 2005.

Curtis, William J. R., **Modern Architecture Since 1900**, Phaidon Press, London, UK, 1982 (3rd edn, revised and expanded, 1996).

Dal Co, Francesco, and Mazzariol, Giuseppe, **Carlo Scarpa: The Complete Works**, Electa Editrice, Milan, Italy, 1984/The Architectural Press, London, UK, 1986.

French, Philip, Frayling, Christopher and Adam, Ken, **Moonraker, Strangelove and other Celluloid Dreams: The Visionary Art of Ken Adam**, edited by David Sylvester, Serpentine Gallery, London, UK, 1999.

Glancey, Jonathan, **C20th Architecture – The Structures That Shaped The Century**, Carlton Books, London, UK, 1998.

Hanson, Matt, **Building Sci-Fi Moviescapes – The Science Behind the Fiction**, Focal Press, an imprint of Elsevier, Burlington, USA, 2005.

Hess, Alan, **Hyperwest – American Residential Architecture on the Edge**, Thames & Hudson, London, UK, 1996.

Hess, Alan, **The Architecture of John Lautner**, Thames & Hudson, London, UK, 1999.

Leitch, Michael (ed), **Your Day at The Lowry**, The Lowry Press, Salford, UK, 2002.

Lyall, Sutherland, **Masters of Structure – Engineering Today's Innovative Buildings**, Laurence King, London, UK, 2002.

McCarter, Robert, **Frank Lloyd Wright**, Phaidon Press, London, UK, 1997.

Melvin, Jeremy, **Isms – Understanding Architecture**, Herbert Press, London, UK, 2005.

Nägeli, Walter, **Zaha Hadid: Vitra Fire Station**, Aedes, Berlin, Germany, 1992.

Pawley, Martin, **Future Systems – The Story of Tomorrow**, Phaidon Press, London, UK, 1993.

Pearman, Hugh, **The Deep – The World's Only Submarium – An Icon for Hull**, Wordsearch, London, UK, 2002.

Petit, Jean, **Niemeyer: Museu de Arte Contemporânea de Niterói**, Editora Revan, Rio de Janeiro, Brazil, 1997.

Powell, Kenneth, **New Architecture in Britain**, Merrell Publishers, London, UK, 2003.

Powell, Kenneth, **Architecture of the Future – Richard Rogers**, edited by Robert Torday, Birkhäuser, Basel, Switzerland, 2006.

Ragheb, J. Fiona (ed), **Frank Gehry – Architect**, Guggenheim Museum Publications/ Harry N. Abrams, New York, USA, 2001.

Slessor, Catherine, **Eco-Tech – Sustainable Architecture and High Technology**, Thames & Hudson, London, UK, 1997.

Sudjic, Deyan, **The Architecture of Richard Rogers**, Blue Print Monograph, Fourth Estate/Word Search, London, UK, 1994.

Topham, Sean, **Where's my Space Age? – The Rise and Fall of Futuristic Design**, Prestel Verlag, Munich, Germany, 2003.

Various, **Carlo Scarpa, Architect: Intervening with History**, introduction by Nicholas Olsberg, Canadian Centre for Architecture, Montréal, Canada/Monacelli Press, New York, USA, 1999.

Weber-Hof, Claudine (ed), **Icons of Architecture – The 20th Century**, Prestel Verlag, Munich, Germany, 1998.

Welsh, John, **Modern House**, Phaidon Press, London, UK, 1995.

Wilhide, Elizabeth, **The Millennium Dome**, Harper Collins, London, UK, 1999.

MAGAZINES & PERIODICALS

Bibliotheca Alexandrina, Alexandria
(see pp 128–31)
Davey, Peter, 'Bibliotheca Alexandrina',
pp 40–51, **The Architectural Review**,
September 2001.

Casa da Musica, Porto (see pp 138–41)
Cohn, David, 'Casa da Musica', pp 100–11,
Architectural Record, USA, July 2005.

Expo Station, Singapore (see pp 120–23)
Chee, Li-Lian, 'Moving Experience', pp 82–85,
World Architecture, no. 95, April 2001.

Dawson, Susan, 'On the right track', pp 4–7,
'Metal Works' supplement, **The Architects'
Journal**, no. 25, vol. 215, 27 February 2002.

Guggenheim, Bilbao (see pp 36–39)
McCrum, Robert, 'Where to go to see a
masterpiece', pp 14–20, **Observer Life
Magazine**, 12 October 1997.

Kunsthaus, Graz (see pp 178–81)
Baillieu, Amanda, 'Hippy cheek', pp 24–32,
RIBA Journal, December 2003.

Lefaivre, Liane, 'Yikes! Peter Cook's and
Colin Fournier's perkily animistic Kunsthaus',
pp 92–99, **Architectural Record**, USA,
January 2004.

The Lowry, Salford (see pp 116–19)
Powell, Kenneth, 'Affairs of the Art', pp 8–9,
The Architects' Journal, no. 1, vol. 212,
6 July 2000.

Sudjic, Deyan, 'I've taken a shine to it',
pp 28–39, **The Observer Review**, 30 April 2000.

Bevan, Robert, 'Technicoloured Dreamboat',
pp 10–14, **Building Design**, 1438, 28 April 2000.

MAC, Niterói, Rio de Janeiro (see pp 150–53)
Oliveira, Luis, 'Planet Niemeyer',
The Architectural Review, April 1999.

Magna Science Adventure Centre, Rotherham
(see pp 124–27)
Bateson, Katherine, 'Magna Opus', pp 14–17,
Building Design, 6 April 2001.

Pople, Nicolas, 'Industrial Revolution', pp
38–46, **RIBA Journal**, April 2001.

Museum of Fruit, Yamanashi (see pp 24–27)
Chow, Phoebe 'Faithful Synthesis', pp 43–47,
The Architectural Review, 1189, March 1996.

Melvin, Jeremy, 'Aliens in the Orchard',
pp 16–17, **Building Design**, 27 October, 1995.

National Centre for Popular Music, Sheffield
(see pp 112–15)
Hatton, Brian, 'Awopbop-allbop-wopbamboom:
an icon for Sheffield', pp 24–30, **Architecture
Today**, no. 97, April 1999.

NatWest Media Centre, Lord's Cricket Ground,
London (see pp 158–61)
Rosenthal, Tim, 'Bowled Over', pp 46–49, **RA
(Royal Academy) Magazine**, no. 74, Spring 2002.

Phaeno Science Centre, Wolfsburg
(see pp 142–45)
Bizley, Graham, 'Zaha's Blinding Science',
pp 16–21, **Building Design**, 1701, 2 December
2005.

Pearson, Clifford A., 'Phaeno Science Center in
Wolfsburg', pp70–81, **Architectural Record**,
USA, February 2006.

Young, Eleanor, 'Natural Phenomenon',
pp 38–46, **RIBA Journal**, 113/1, January 2006.

The Shack, Northamptonshire (see pp 28–31)
Davey, Peter, 'Wildlife Retreat', Design Review
Section, pp 36–38, **The Architectural Review**,
September 1998.

Scottish Parliament, Edinburgh (see pp 84–87)
Cohn, David, 'EMBT and RMJM's bittersweet
masterpiece', pp 98–111, **Architectural Record**,
USA, February 2005.

Wright, Clare, 'Slàinte!', pp 26–38, **RIBA
Journal**, 111/10, October 2004.

Selfridges, Birmingham (see pp 174–77)
Evans, Barrie, 'Model Answer', pp 28–43,
The Architects' Journal, no. 13, vol. 218,
9 October 2003.

Russell, James S., AIA, 'Future System's
curvaceous outpost', pp 234–41, **Architectural
Record**, USA, June 2004.

Swiss RE, 30 St. Mary Axe, London
(see pp 182–85)
Russell, James S., AIA, '30 St. Mary Axe',
pp 218–27, **Architectural Record**, USA,
June 2004

Sudjic, Deyan (ed), 'Foster in London',
pp 14–17, **Domus**, no. 865, Suplemento A, 2003.

Conclusion (see pp 186–87)
Knutt, Elaine, 'Robots to build homes', pp 1 &
19, **Building Design**, 1707m, 3 February 2006.

RECOMMENDED FILMS

There are many cinematic references used to
describe the architecture featured in this book,
which is hardly surprising given that many of
them have been used as film sets since their
completion. This small selection of films offers
a starting point for anyone wishing to explore
for themselves the complex and seemingly
symbiotic relationship between real and
cinematic worlds.

Alien, directed by Ridley Scott, 1979.

Aliens, directed by James Cameron, 1986.

Blade Runner, directed by Ridley Scott, 1982.

Buck Rogers, directed by Ford Beebe and Saul
A. Goodkind, 1939.

**Doctor Strangelove or How I Learned to Stop
Worrying and Love the Bomb**, directed by
Stanley Kubrick, 1964.

Gattaca, directed by Andrew Niccol, 1997.

Flash Gordon, directed by Mike Hodges, 1980.

Stargate, directed by Roland Emmerich, 1984.

Star Wars Episode IV – A New Hope, directed
by George Lucas, 1977.

**Star Wars Episode V – The Empire Strikes
Back**, directed by George Lucas, 1980.

Star Wars Episode VI – The Return of the Jedi,
directed by George Lucas, 1983.

Tron, directed by Steven Lisberger, 1982.

Metropolis, directed by Fritz Lang, 1927.

Acknowledgments

Once upon a time, in a picture library far, far away, a young picture researcher assembled a collection of twenty architectural images that he thought could conceivably be entitled 'Building Science Fiction'. The collection grew and an idea grew with it until the point when it was ready to leave the database and become something more than an idea; a fully fledged book of over two hundred images, with many more words to go with them.

I would like to thank Lynne and Richard Bryant of Arcaid for creating the kind of working environment where such ideas are nurtured, for their company has constantly fed my imagination ever since I began to sort through its many files.

I must also single out architect Bart Prince for his very generous correspondence, full of the kind of details that make his discipline the fascinating craft that it is.

Photographer Bill Tingey, with his well-travelled knowledge of Japan, was another invaluable collaborator in my research.

And last, but by no means least, I must thank Arcaid's photographers on mass, through whose skilfully trained lenses I have been privileged to witness a world less ordinary. This is their book as much as mine.

Paul Cattermole, May 2006

Notes

1 AD100, **Architectural Digest**, USA, January 2002.
2 'Ideals', Kendrick Bangs Kellogg, www.kendrickbangskellogg.com
3 Excerpts from 'Hernández's House', a poem by A. Hernández Navarro.
4 Ibid.
5 **The Millennium Dome**, Elizabeth Wilhide, p. 37.